"HAPPY DAYS" IN FRANCE & FLANDERS

"HAPPY DAYS"
IN FRANCE & FLANDERS WITH THE 47TH AND 49TH DIVISIONS BY BENEDICT WILLIAMSON WITH AN INTRODUCTION BY LIEUT.-COL. R. C. FEILDING, D.S.O.

MCMXXI

Harding & More Ltd
The Ambrosden Press
119 High Holborn, London, W.C.1

To the boys of
THE 47th & 49th DIVISIONS

CONTENTS

	PAGE
INTRODUCTION BY R. C. FEILDING, D.S.O.	xi

CHAPTER I
TO THE FLANDERS FRONT . . 1

CHAPTER II
AT A CASUALTY CLEARING STATION 6

CHAPTER III
FIRST DAYS WITH THE DUKE OF WELLINGTON'S 16

CHAPTER IV
AT NIEUPORT 24

CHAPTER V
QUIET DAYS AT LA PANNE . . 40

CHAPTER VI
THE STRUGGLE FOR PASSCHENDAELE 49

CHAPTER VII
ON THE MENIN ROAD . . . 65

CHAPTER VIII
FIRST LEAVE AND MENIN ROAD AGAIN 77

CHAPTER IX
ON THE SOMME FRONT . . 81

CHAPTER X
THE MARCH OFFENSIVE . . . 96

CHAPTER XI
AT BOUZINCOURT 114

CHAPTER XII
IN THE TRENCHES BEFORE ALBERT 127

CHAPTER XIII
THE GREAT ADVANCE . . . 143

CHAPTER XIV
SHOT AT DAWN 157

CONTENTS

CHAPTER XV
THE ADVANCE THROUGH LILLE AND TOURNAI 161

CHAPTER XVI
HOW THE END CAME ON THE WESTERN FRONT 178

CHAPTER XVII
AFTERWARDS 186

INDEX 193

☘ INTRODUCTION ☘

THE life of a British Army chaplain on the Western Front was almost what he himself chose to make it, but to succeed in the rôle required a superman. A true vocation, coupled with rare insensibility, courage, and almost inhuman tact, could alone carry him through.

He wore the insignia of an officer, but, as no place was assigned to him either in the line or out of it, he was, in a sense, Pariah among the officers of the battalions which he served. From the men he was separated by the official barrier which his commissioned rank entailed.

Being without status, our padres were usually relegated to a field ambulance, whence—according to temperament—they could pursue their avocation assiduously, as they generally did, in spite of the handicap of the distance which divided them from their flock, or live a life of comparative ease at a comfortable distance behind the line.

Father Benedict, the writer of the following pages, possessed a personality which will ever remain a happy memory to those who knew him in the War. The most zealous of priests, the most human of men, he rejoiced in the atmosphere of the trenches—in the proximity of the forward troops. For there he found selflessness supreme. There, on a scale so grand as perhaps to surpass anything experienced before in the history of mankind, he saw the spirit of self-sacrifice incarnate—the essence of Christ's teaching made practical. Such is the influence of the shells!

He was known in the 47th Division—in which the writer of this preface served with him—by the nickname of "Happy Days," on account of his unquenchable optimism. He seemed to live in a world of sunshine, destitute of shadows. He carried out his duties as he faced the sordid horrors of the battlefields with a child-like simplicity, inspiring the living, and comforting with his faith the parting moments of many a dying soldier.

His diary, which is printed practically as it was written, contributes further first-hand evidence as to the wonderful qualities of our men—their never-failing cheerfulness under the most appalling circumstances; their bravery; the complete absence of rancour with which they fought. As Father Benedict says, "During all my experience on the front, even when the enemy was raining his shells on us, I have never heard an expression of hatred uttered by our boys."

He tells how the British soldier took his medicine. Indeed, poor fellow, is he not still doing so—in many cases half starving in our streets—in the same quiet way in which he took it in the trenches?

Father Benedict says " the fortitude and sublime self-sacrifice and endurance of the men should surely remind people of their duty to the ex-soldier."

May the publication of this book awaken, in those of its readers who may still need a reminder, a true sense of their responsibilities—that the debt which England has contracted may be redeemed in full!

ROWLAND C. FEILDING, D.S.O.

TWYFORD, HANTS.

CHAPTER I

TO THE FLANDERS FRONT

EARLSFIELD lies in the south-west of London on the low-lying land between Clapham and Wimbledon, a waste of one-storied houses, all possessed of a singular sameness, and Garratt Lane winds through the centre.

Just near the station and back from the road stands St. Gregory's, with nothing outwardly attractive about it, but once you have passed inside you enter an austere other-world atmosphere in strange contrast with all you see without. The great stone columns with their massive cushioned caps, the soaring baldachino covering the high altar, give an impression of solemnity that steadily grows as the building becomes more familiar.

Very early on the morning of May 22nd in 1917, just as the first light of dawn was beginning to creep through the windows and cast its fitful shadows on column and roof, I said my last Mass in England before setting out for the Western Front. A few friends had gathered round the altar, appearing like shadows in the uncertain light, I spoke a few words of farewell, breakfast, and then off to Victoria to take train for France. The leave-train—well, everybody knows it: the little groups talking inconsequent nothings to cover up their real feelings; the sense, never absent but never expressed, that the parting may be final; "Good-bye, and the best of luck!"; and the train is gliding out of the station almost before one perceives it. There is silence all the way down, only broken as the train runs alongside the embarkation quay on the pier at Folkestone.

Father Charles Murphy, who was expecting to

follow me to France any day, and a few friends gathered on the platform to say good-bye.

On our arrival at Folkestone we had to wait till 4 o'clock before embarking, so we scattered over the town to pass the time. The day was warm and oppressive, with a little rain falling occasionally, a mist hanging over the sea, through which at intervals the sun strove to cast its rays fitfully.

The boom of guns now and then rolled in towards the shore from somewhere far out in the Channel.

Folkestone looked much as it always has, save for the crowds of khaki everywhere. A long column of W.A.A.C.s on a route-march passed us, all looking very smart in their new khaki uniforms, moving along at a good swinging pace.

About 3 o'clock we turned once more to the embarkation office, and thence to the boat. It was just the usual crowd of officers and men returning from leave, a few nurses, half a dozen W.A.A.C.s, all very silent, as is always the case with the returning leave-boat. At half-past four we steamed out of the harbour, with a torpedo-destroyer on either side, and one of the small naval airships in front. We reached Boulogne at half-past seven.

Father Woodlocke, S.J., met our party on the landing-stage, and took us to the Hôtel Louvre, where we spent the night.

The next morning we made our way to the office of the Chaplains' Department. One after another we went in and received our orders; I remember Father Trail, one of the oldest members of our party, coming out very distressed because he was appointed to a base hospital, instead of up the line.

My orders were to go to No. 10 casualty clearing

station to attend the wounded there during the attack on Messines Ridge. The train was to leave next morning, so most of us spent the day looking round the city and making a few last purchases.

Next morning, May 24th, I said Mass early in a fine old church across the quay, and at 9.30 the troop train moved out of the station. A silent company, for all the officers were returning from leave, and there was the strange stillness that always hangs over the returning leave-train. Everyone knows to what they are going back, and their thoughts are far away with the dear ones left behind.

Soon after midday we arrived at Calais and got a really excellent lunch at the buffet for a very reasonable price; the food shortage had not yet made itself felt as it did later on in the War.

I went off to find our two Sisters Eileen and Hilda Staunton, at the Anglo-Belgian Hospital No. 2, but missed them; they were both on night duty.

One of my companions was a young flying officer, just going up to join the Squadron at Abeele. "There is the front line," said one of our company to me as we came in sight of Mont des Cats.

To the surprise of all, the train made the journey in quite record time, and we drew into Poperinghe station at half-past four.

Just across the road facing the station was a small ted brick chateau known to all as "The Officers' Rest": it had not been open long then, and was in the initial stage of development, but tea was available, and later on a very fair dinner. The house was already a great boon to those going to or returning from leave, especially as it was so near the station. The front was extremely quiet as I stood on the platform waiting for a train to take me down to Remi siding where the four casualty clearing stations were erected.

A peaceful spring evening, calm and restful, the sun just setting in the west, and except for the observation balloons and some wrecked buildings near the station, no sign of war.

A few soldiers were standing about; I had just remarked to the corporal on duty: "It is so quiet you would hardly believe there was a war on," and received the answer: "A great deal too quiet for my liking," when the silence was broken by the boom of a gun, and the shrill shriek of a shell directly overhead. The men scattered for shelter, and gathered again, laughing, immediately after.

Where did it go? "It was a dud." A few minutes more, another shriek and a terrific crash as the shell burst behind the station. This was not a dud. Then they came crashing over in quick succession; the town soon became hidden from view in the clouds of dust from falling buildings. One shell fell close to the rails, sending up a vast cloud of dust and smoke, and the fragments began to fall around.

Our train drew up, we scrambled into the cattle trucks, and by and by we slowly moved out of the station. Looking back, the shells were still falling; a turn in the line and Poperinghe was out of sight.

A little while and the train drew up at the siding. Long lines of huts stretched out on either side. I dropped down on to the track, the soldiers giving a hand with the baggage, and then went ahead to find No. 10 casualty clearing station. I discovered the orderly room and met Colonel Marriott, who was in charge of the hospital. He took me over to the mess, on the other side of the railway, for dinner. "You will have to sleep in one of the wards to-night," he said; "to-morrow we will arrange for your quarters." The mess was a spacious building crowded with officers.

After dinner I returned to one of the officers' wards, where the sister had a bed arranged for me. I was just thinking of rest when I was called to attend Captain Merriman, who had been badly wounded during the shelling at Poperinghe that evening. He was conscious and in good spirits. I anointed him with the holy oils and then returned to spend my first night on the Western Front. It was fairly quiet, except for a few shells going over; but they were falling well away from us.

CHAPTER II

AT A CASUALTY CLEARING STATION

THE next day I moved into one of the little corrugated iron huts which formed the officers' quarters. My orderly soon improvised a bed by means of a stretcher, some blankets, and my valise; a few boards and trestles provided a table, and in a short time the hut was transformed into quite a comfortable little room. The country round was characteristically Flemish: away on the left the towers and spires of Poperinghe showed through the trees, while beyond the long range of hospital wards, across the railway, Mont Rouge and Mont Noir with their windmills, and further along Mont des Cats with its monastic church crowning the height, completed a pleasant prospect. Here I spent one of the happiest and most fruitful months of my time in France. I had come up in anticipation of the long-prepared attack on Messines Ridge. All the medical and nursing staffs of the four clearing stations had been doubled, numbers of extra wards had been erected; in fact, everything had been so well planned and foreseen that both during the strenuous days preceding and following, as well as on the actual day itself, staff and accommodation proved more than sufficient to meet every demand made upon them.

The heavy artillery bombardment in the days and nights preceding the attack never for a moment ceased, the steady regular roll of the guns went on without cessation, and as evening fell the whole front was lit up with the brilliant flashes, occasionally varied by more striking illuminations as some ammunition dump was fired, and went up in a splendid blaze of light.

The artillery suffered heavily from gas and counter-battery work, and every day I saw the wounded brought down in great numbers on the ambulance cars from the advanced dressing stations.

The work in these great temporary hospitals—for that is what the C.C.S.s really are—was admirably organised, and everything possible done to alleviate the lot of the wounded.

As the ambulances quickly discharged their load, the bearers carried them through the reception hut, where their particulars were taken, to the ward next the large operating theatre for the surgical cases, or farther down to other wards, if not destined for the operating theatre. Here the orderlies were at hand with water and fresh bandages, and the patient was with wonderful speed comfortably settled in bed, receiving whatever food or drink his particular injury allowed.

In the C.C.S. perhaps more than anywhere else the full horror of war is brought home to the observer, for while the regimental aid post only gathers in the casualties of the regiment, and the advanced dressing station generally only the wounded of one or at most two brigades, through the C.C.S. stream all the wounded from a whole corps battle front.

And every day, both before and after the battle, saw at least several hundred cases enter each of the four C.C.S.s, while on the day itself the wounded numbered thousands.

I can never forget those days and nights at Remi siding. It was generally after dark that the majority of the wounded came down, owing to the difficulty of getting ambulances along the shelled roads while it was light. If our artillery was active, the enemy's was certainly no less so, though the total of our guns considerably outnumbered his; and if we suffered on our side, he must have suffered far more.

As soon as night fell the ambulances began to roll in, and the regular tramp of the stretcher-bearers along the duckboards announced the coming of a fresh convoy. The light falls fitfully from the shaded lamps on the long line of stretchers with their blood-stained burdens that quickly fills the ward. Orderlies and sisters go silently about their duties. Here is the work of war in all its ghastly horror. Men disfigured and blackened beyond recognition, shattered and battered, a mass of blood and wounds, yet most of them are conscious and able to speak a little, and dictate a few words to their loved ones at home, or ask for a drink of water to cool their parched lips.

Some are Catholics, and grateful for the sight of a priest, and eager to receive the rites of the Church. At night I carried the Blessed Sacrament as well as the holy oils, so they had the consolation of receiving Our Blessed Lord. Amongst them were some old members of St. Gregory's.

Their restraint is wonderful: it is rarely that a cry or a groan escapes the sufferers, and then it is half suppressed; for despite their agony, they are full of thought for others, and anxious not to trouble or disturb their neighbours.

Nothing, indeed, was so striking in my experience there as the splendid way "our boys" bore their agonies of pain, some of them so young as to seem mere children, and yet no word of complaint; and for any little service, so much gratitude. At night, as I have gone the round of the long line of wards, one came across men wide awake, unable to find rest or sleep in any position, and yet holding themselves in from even a groan lest they should disturb the rest of their more fortunate neighbours.

And what shall I say of the amazing devotion of the sisters, ever cheerful and smiling, never wearied by any labour, seemingly almost superhuman in the unsparing way they gave themselves to the service of our boys. The work of the Territorial Nursing Sisters can never be adequately praised—it was beyond all praise.

Women's work in other departments has been splendid too; but the first place must be given to these sisters, whose heroic self-sacrifice brought back to life thousands of our boys, and whose sympathy and gentleness soothed the last hours of the many who have gone to their " last home."

It is the grey uniform of the nursing sisters that will ever be held in grateful veneration and unforgetable remembrance by the vast host of soldier boys who know all the magnificent service they rendered; who owe their lives to the ceaseless watchfulness that never grew weary and never grew tired.

Of their courage under fire; of their entire self-forgetfulness in danger; and devotion to duty, the list of awards gives some feeble clue; but the decorated are only the few out of the thousands who have performed deeds of equal devotion and service.

And again, the work of the doctors in the operation wards, hour after hour of patient toil, the last case receiving exactly the same care as the first: how often have I watched them as each poor mangled body was laid on the table, the deft hands, gentle, swift, skilful; the watchful eye, the unsparing devotion—service which makes little show, yet as straining and exhausting as any endured in the battle line.

So the days sped on, the human loads came down, the sisters and doctors never tiring at their great work.

What a contradiction war is. Less than a few miles away there is a line of men engaged in the work of destroying and mutilating each other; over these very wards sometimes the shells go singing on their way to do their work of destruction farther back; and here is a line of men and women striving to mend the bleeding, broken victims that stream back from that forward line.

As the day drew near for the great attack, the artillery duel grew in volume and strength, and I fell asleep each night to the steady pulsation of the guns, even and regular as the engines of some great liner.

The number of victims increased too; gas casualties came in—a pitiful sight indeed, strong men battling desperately for breath, a brief struggle, and then the great silence. I remember one night a fine man and a frail young boy, both suffering terribly, both making a brave fight for existence. In the morning I went over; the man had gone during the night, the boy whom we scarcely thought could last an hour was still battling for life. Each morning as I went round I expected to find the lad gone; but no, he held on, gradually gained strength, and to the surprise of all, was finally well enough to be evacuated.

One of the great events of the day was, of course, the Red Cross train; how eagerly the patients looked for the day when they could be either carried or walk to the train. No holiday train in peace-time was ever awaited so eagerly, or stirred so much gladness, as the " Blighty train," as it was popularly called.

" Is it a Blighty ? " was the invariable question of every wounded man, as the doctor or sister bent over him to look at his wound, and the assurance that it was gave the man peace and contentment, however great his pain. I remember a major who was down as a stretcher case one day, and had to be left behind because all the lying cases had been filled, determined to take no risks of another disappointment. Next morning he managed to get on his feet somehow, and was out waiting for the train, resolved nothing on earth should keep him behind this time.

Each morning I used to make my way along the railway to the farm-house where a little chapel had been fitted up by the efforts of the Catholic chaplains. After the Mass I went through the wards giving Holy Communion to all the Catholic boys able to receive. The sisters were always quick to have everything in readiness and to render any help they could ; and, indeed, the whole time I always received every help and assistance from the sisters in seeing to the spiritual needs of our boys, and if ever a dangerous case came in during the night, a message always called me to the ward at once.

Sometimes our night would be disturbed by the anti-aircraft guns, and we could see the enemy planes, flying very high, caught in the search-lights with the white puffs of bursting shrapnel around.

The shelling, too, of Poperinghe, and the country between, went on with clockwork regularity, the most serious event for us being the occasion when a shell bursting in front of the door of the cottage of the good family who did all our washing, they determined then and there to take their departure for some safer sphere, and we were left—with the dirty clothes. One day I set out to see the air squadrons at Abeele, and make arrangements for the men to go to their duties and receive Holy Communion. The roads were crowded with guns and munitions pressing up on their way to their positions. I looked in at the parish church on the way, where Benediction was being given. Here I found two soldiers just going up into the line, anxious for Confession and Communion. I heard their confessions, they received Holy Communion, and went their way not a little consoled. They had scarcely hoped for such an opportunity. The flying officers gathered the Catholics together in one of the sheds, where all were able to receive the Sacraments.

The great day dawned at last, and the roll of the guns reached its highest pitch during the early hours of the morning, and then came silence. The attack was one of the most brilliant successes of the War. The first wounded were streaming in about 10 o'clock. They came down in ever-increasing numbers until evening, when the climax was reached; but there was no delay and no overcrowding—the preparations were perfect. Through the night and next day the numbers coming down remained very much the same, and then they gradually subsided to the normal standard, although the artillery casualties increased steadily during the days following the capture of the ridge.

The trains were drawn up waiting, and as soon as one was filled and drew off another drew in, so that in a remarkably short time after the action the great majority of the wounded had passed down to the hospitals at the Base and through to England.

There were strange contrasts. One day, as I was in the ward with the gassed men, struggling and dying, came shouts and cheers from the great field at the side of the C.C.S. where the various ambulances were having their sports day. The wounded able to move or to be carried out were seated round the field and joined in the excitement and cheering of the crowd. Races, greasy pole, high-jump, etc.—all the usual events filled up the programme, and while the shouts of the spectators rent the air, men were dying in the wards near by.

Out of harmony, as it may appear, with the surroundings, such occasional relief as this was absolutely necessary to ease the ceaseless strain of the ambulance workers. It was a brief respite from the horror ever streaming back from the front. The German wounded included a number of Polish soldiers from Prussian Poland, all Catholics, who eagerly welcomed the priest, and gave every sign of gratitude, kissing the priest's stole after receiving the Sacraments. Most of them were mortally wounded, and died within a few hours of their arrival.

The sad side of war was sometimes relieved by amusing incidents. In one of the worst wards, where few recovered, a young Deptford boxer was brought in from the operating theatre, still under the influence of the anæsthetic. First the boy was directing a boxing match, and kept the ward laughing with his caustic remarks to the combatants in delightful Cockney language, then he was instructing a bayonet squad.

First he gave a little preliminary address and then the exercise was in motion: " Hi, you there! if you don't look alive he'll be in front and do you in. Now, then, there, you, bash him, tread on him, get yer bayonet out, all's fair in love and war." So the stream of comments flowed on.

Then apparently the show was over, and he addresses a question to his squad : " Anyone know the spirit of the bayonet? What, none of yer know?—you, there, don't you know?—no, not one of yer knows. I'll tell yer, the spirit of the bayonet is ter kill—ter kill—ter kill." I never saw that sad ward in so merry a mood as it was that day. I am glad to say the boy made good progress and was able to take his way to Blighty.

It was sad to watch the steady growth of the long rows of white crosses in the cemetery beside the C.C.S. Every day we laid to rest some sixteen to twenty men, and during the attack and for some days following the number rose to an average of seventy.

Very pathetic was the sight of the line of figures, each rolled in an Army blanket, lying beside the open graves. When a few months later I visited the same cemetery, the crosses had increased by something like a thousand. It helped one to realise what our losses were like when one reflected that this was only one cemetery amongst many, besides all the smaller enclosures scattered over the front.

My time at the C.C.S. came swiftly to a close. Father Rawlinson had been down on a visit to the salient and told me I might expect to go to a Division very soon. On June 25th the order came to join the 49th Division. Regretfully I bade farewell to the C.C.S. and went once again to Poperinghe, whence I took train to Hazebrouck.

I must mention one other incident that befell at the C.C.S. before I left it: the enemy was heavily shelling the back areas during the last days I was there, and a considerable number of badly wounded kept coming in. Some wounded Munsters came in one night and told me Father Maloney had been brought down wounded in the ambulance: " Shure, the boys will all die without him; do find out how he is," said they, forgetful of their own wounds in their concern for the fate of their loved Padre. I found he was in the Canadian C.C.S. adjoining and hastened round at once. He had just recovered consciousness. I learned that he had been blown up by a high explosive shell in Dickebusch. Some of those who were standing with him were killed instantly: but although blown up nearly 20 feet in the air he had no wound. Of course he was badly shaken and some bones broken by the fall, but that he escaped so lightly was little short of a miracle.

CHAPTER III

FIRST DAYS WITH THE DUKE OF WELLINGTON'S

EVERYONE knows what a move is like on the Western Front. You go to your station to report to the R.T.O., he sends you on a few stations to report to another R.T.O., who refers you to another, and at the end of a few days you reach your destination, which in normal times you could have reached in as many hours. The R.T.O. is generally a much worried individual, very stiff and official in manner, and not too helpful. Of course there are R.T.O.s and R.T.O.s, but on a liberal computation the number of really good R.T.O.s was, according to the opinion of the Army in France, exceedingly small. The trains certainly now moved at a more rapid pace than they did in the early days of the War, when, except for the look of the thing, one might as well have walked.

However, I got along in a fairly comfortable carriage with only the door and some of the windows missing, which, as the weather was warm and fine, did not greatly matter.

Arrived at Hazebrouck, I found the only chance to get further forward was to travel in one of the trucks of a supply train. I had some hours to wait for this and managed to get a meal of sorts at the station, then had a look round the town, as yet undamaged by shell fire. Towards five the supply train set off, and I landed at Berquette. Another train took me on to La Gorgue, where I was told the 49th Divisional Headquarters were established. The station was out in the country, so leaving my baggage there, I walked down to the town and found the headquarters at a fairly good château in the principal street. General Percival and Major Duckworth received me with great kindness, speedily procured a meal, and gave me a hearty welcome to the Division. After supper they found me a billet, and that night I had the first sleep in a real bed since I came out.

The next morning I said Mass in the parish church, a fine spacious structure, built during the early days of the Gothic revival, the general lines and much of the detail excellent, and only very slightly damaged. The next morning I motored over to Zelobes, where I joined the 1/2nd West Riding Field Ambulance for a few days until I got my final posting. I found some sort of a place to sleep in for the night, which was a fairly quiet one.

The ambulance headquarters were situated in a large seventeenth-century farm-house in very pleasant surroundings. Here I met Father Adamson, S.J., who later on was gassed up at Nieuport, and Father Doyle, whom I was succeeding.

All around there were evidences of the effect of war, especially in the case of the churches: the one at La Fosse was completely wrecked, as well as those of several other villages in the neighbourhood.

The weather during my stay at Zelobes was extremely fine, so I was able to spend my day out visiting the various units of my brigade, and others in the neighbourhood. In my wanderings I called on a labour battalion, whose C.O. was no lover of Padres. Without being in the least aware of it, I found I was the third Catholic Chaplain to call that day. "What!" said the testy old gentleman, "another of them? There's been two here to-day already." "Well," I said, "I am the third." However, in spite of the unfavourable reception, he sent all the Catholics of his battalion to Mass on Sunday.

The Portuguese troops were just coming up to take over on this front, and as they were always calling on the artillery, the nights were very lively and the whole sky brilliantly lit up with the gun-flashes.

On my first Sunday I said one Mass in a room of one of the cottages at Zelobes, and then walked out to Lestrem, where I said Mass for our Catholic boys at 10 o'clock: a fair congregation assembled in the quaint old mediaeval church, including a large contingent from the before-mentioned labour company. The church was packed at the parish Mass, which immediately followed ours, with a most devout congregation, practically the whole population of the village being present. This part of the country was, from a religious point of view, exceedingly good. At night I went to Benediction given by Father Adamson for his brigade, in a little temporary chapel erected by the curé at Fosse. The old-time hymns were sung to the accompaniment of the roll of guns without, and the whole service, very short and simple, was most impressive.

I spent my days going round visiting our troops, who were dispersed in Paradis, Merville, and other villages around. The long walks in the glorious sunshine through pleasant lanes and fields were very exhilarating, and by visiting the men in their billets, one gradually became known to all in the brigade.

My orders came on July 5th to join the 1/5th of the West Ridings, or, as they preferred to be known themselves, " the Duke of Wellington's," at Paradis. I walked over and saw the commander, Colonel Tew, a man whom one grew to appreciate each day the more as we became better acquainted; a silent man, keeping much to himself, but a fine soldier whom all felt they could trust absolutely. It was arranged I should live at the transport officers' mess, which then included the quartermaster and the French interpreter. A limber came over for my belongings, and so I went over to Paradis and took up my residence in a room at the village school house. In my wanderings in the country I made it a point to go into any place where I found troops and see what Catholics were there, and if they had no chaplain of their own, arrange that they had an opportunity of approaching the Sacraments; in this way all sorts of units were able to fulfil their duties.

Sunday, July 8th, was my first Sunday with the brigade, and the church, a fair example of the modern Gothic style, very well kept, was filled at the Mass, at which I gave general absolution and Communion in view of our possibly soon going into the line. Being mostly Yorkshire men, the singing of the hymns during the Mass was excellent, and I arranged Benediction and Communion in the afternoon for those who had been unable to hear Mass in the morning.

Before the end of the week the order came for the division to move, and our pleasant stay at Paradis came to an end. The troops were very popular with the village folk, and everyone was in the street to see us march off on Friday morning, *en route* for Merville. By the time we arrived at the station we were fairly warm and perspiring.

The entraining did not take long, and we were soon on our way to Dunkerque, which we reached about 8 o'clock in the evening. We formed up outside the station and marched out to St. Pol-sur-la-Mer. We had quite an enthusiastic reception, the streets being lined with people to see us come in, and during our short stay we received the greatest kindness and consideration from everyone. We were encamped in a field on the side of the road, and as the supply of tents was rather limited, we were very crowded.

The brigadier, General Lewis, sent for me the next morning, to arrange for the Catholics in the brigade to get an opportunity of receiving the Sacraments on the following Sunday, as we were expecting to go up to the attack at Nieuport soon after.

The church at St. Pol was a well-conceived building in the style of the thirteenth century, consisting of aisles, nave, and apsidal sanctuary, transepts with a fine west tower and spire. The interior was lofty and spacious, decorated in excellent taste; the stained glass of quite a good type.

On Sunday, July 15th, I said Mass for all our brigade: the troops filled the church, a young lady member of the congregation played the great organ, the men sang the hymns magnificently, and the great stream of communicants made the service one of the most inspiring of any at which I have assisted out in France.

Indeed, I shall never forget that day: the long lines of men kneeling at the altar rails, intensely devout and recollected, line succeeding line, and as one reflected that for many it must be the last time, it made the occasion a very moving one. It was an immense consolation to find such a splendid spirit of earnest devotion animating the Catholics of the brigade. I heard many confessions in the afternoon, and after Benediction gave Holy Communion to those who had been prevented from coming in the morning.

On Monday I paid a short visit to Dunkerque, and saw the fine old flamboyant church, badly damaged, as well as many houses in the town, by the fire of the long-range guns. Tuesday was spent in hearing confessions and giving Holy Communion. We said good-bye to the warm-hearted and hospitable people of St. Pol with regret, and retired to rest early, as we had to rise at 3 o'clock next morning to begin our march northward. We had breakfast at 3.30 and began our march at 4.20; even at that early hour quite a number of people had arisen to bid us farewell and wish us God-speed.

The weather was overcast and rain falling most of the time, as we marched along the canal banks with the sand-dunes on the other side, till we reached Bray dunes about 9 o'clock: here we crossed the canal and entered the old Belgian camp.

We were very pleased at securing two tents, and I was just falling off into a pleasant sleep, well content that the tent was the less crowded, when I heard the interpreter's voice: " They have lost their tent." We got up half dressed and turned out into the driving wind and rain, to see what help we could give. The quartermaster was outside struggling with the ropes, the transport officer, buried beneath the canvas, was striving to raise the pole; we set to work to drive in the pegs, but the sand proved treacherous, and as soon as we had secured one side, the wind caught it and over the tent would go again.

After a fruitless struggle, we decided to sleep in the one tent that remained erect, the valises were all dragged out from under the canvas and we got under shelter as quickly as possible. It did not take long for us to fall asleep, and we never woke till late the following morning. One day's rest here, and we were off again, this time to Ghyvelde, where we arrived about 7 o'clock. Here I was billeted at the curé's house, where the colonel was also staying. At Ghyvelde we remained until we moved up into the front line. I went round to all the units in the neighbourhood, found a large number of Australian artillery without a chaplain, and arranged for them to come to us on the Sunday.

On Sunday the church was filled for Mass; I had many confessions and Communions, both from our own men and the Australian troops in the neighbourhood. News came from the front of the first use of the mustard gas up at Nieuport; the earlier reports were alarming indeed, over a thousand men were said to have gone down blinded for life. Happily this proved to be greatly exaggerated, the great majority recovered their sight in a few days; but the danger was a new one, and the permanent effects of the new gas were as yet unknown.

Unfortunately, before we left the Nieuport front the total gas casualties amounted to nearly four thousand, of which about four hundred proved fatal.

On Monday I gave Holy Communion to the men of the 7th Battalion, who were going up into the line the following day, owing to the heavy losses the brigade in front of us had sustained. We were busy three days practising the attack which we were to carry out, as we expected, in a few days' time, but which, in point of fact, never came off.

CHAPTER IV

AT NIEUPORT

NONE of the men who were on the Nieuport front can ever forget our days up there; it became a saying: "Any port in a storm, but *not* Nieuport," for Nieuport in a concentrated form combined all the horrors of the Ypres front, with a number of special features all its own.

I had promised to all our boys going up into the trenches that they should have Holy Communion there every two or three days, as far as it was possible to reach them, and that they should have the Blessed Sacrament in the line somewhere with them.

I went over to Coxyde on Tuesday, where the divisional chaplain, Major Patterson, had called us together to arrange for our positions during the time in the line. Coxyde, a very pleasantly situated seaside place that had sprung into existence in quite recent years, had been rather badly knocked about by the recent shelling, but the sea front had suffered comparatively little injury. Father Guinness was up at Nieuport, working with that single-hearted devotion which characterised him throughout the War, and it was arranged I should go up and relieve him in a few days' time, especially because, owing to Father Adamson having been gassed, much extra work had fallen upon him. Just as I got back to Ghyvelde I met the 7th Battalion going up to the line. The other troops turned out to give them a good send-off.

On Friday, having said Mass early, I set out to the line to take Holy Communion to our men of the 7th Battalion. Accompanied by my servant, O'Grady, a very loyal and devoted boy, I made my way along the canal bank and on through Adinkerke, which was already beginning to show signs of considerable damage from enemy fire. The way proved longer than I had expected, and as we went on the desolation of war became more and more manifest, the gun-fire more violent, and the road entirely deserted, so we had to give up all hope of jumping a lorry. At one of the crossings we met one of the military police, who told us we should get no lorries, as the road was under direct observation. "There is another way up," said he, "but I don't think they will bother about two men. I think you had better keep on." Nieuport came in view at last, and at first sight did not seem to show such signs of ruin and destruction as we had been led to expect; but as we approached nearer, the extent of the damage became more evident. We crossed the canal, made our way into the city, and what a city it was! We climbed up over the masses of débris that filled the streets, now fallen from the shattered buildings on either side; only those who have seen its utter desolation can form any idea of the impression it made upon us. No sign of life in its deserted streets, only the shriek and crash of shells bursting amid the ruins. My servant had spoken hopefully of finding some military police to direct us to the "Redan" where our men were holding the trenches, but we went up one street and down another, stumbling over heaps of brickwork, and keeping our eyes open against shells and falling buildings, without seeing a soul. At last we turned a corner and caught sight of a khaki uniform; it was like catching sight of port on a stormy sea. We made our way towards him and got the direction:

"Go straight down the trench there in the middle of that street, through the tunnel, and then out over the bridge: the Redan is just the other side of the river." We made our way along, came out of the tunnel, and found the ground down to the floating footbridge ploughed and reploughed with shell-holes. The houses that had once stood there had been blown completely away. We got down on to the narrow floating bridge and across to the other side. I went across with comparative unconcern, for I did not know that the bridge was marked down at both ends by 5·9 guns, and shrapnel bursts were sent over in the middle; for as it happened at the moment of crossing, the enemy was relatively quiet.

We reached the famous "Rubber House," a fairly large and strongly fortified concrete building in which the battalions had their headquarters. It was well past 2 o'clock when we arrived, and we had been on our feet since early morning. After a short rest the C.O. gave me a runner, and I went round the trenches hearing the boys' confessions and giving Holy Communion. The trenches were very narrow and contracted, with just space enough for one to pass, and I remember remarking at the time the trenches looked none too strong, as was abundantly proved later on when the enemy's heavy barrage blew them to pieces.

The day was perfect, the sun shining brilliantly, and yet amidst what extraordinary surroundings the men knelt in the trenches to receive their Lord! Shells singing and shrapnel bursting, yet they came with all the quiet devotion with which they are wont to receive Holy Communion at home. It took some three hours to make the round of the front line, and when I got back to headquarters, some tea before setting out on the homeward journey was very welcome. While we were having tea the enemy's shells began to fall around the building, and all fairly heavy stuff, too. An old sergeant was going back with us, and when I reached the opening I was greeted with, " It's no good going out in this, we shall have to wait a bit," as if it was just a shower of rain. We waited and the shelling died down a little. " I think we can get along now, sir." So off we set, but before we could reach the bridge the storm revived, and we had to seek shelter in one of the improvised dugouts that at least gave shelter from the pieces. Twice our shelter was struck and splinters fell through on us, but no one was touched. As the shell struck the dugout a voice out of the darkness exclaimed, " I never prayed in all my life like I have up here." After a while the old sergeant had a look round, and then up at the sky as if it was weather and not shells he was considering. " Are you ready to make a dash for it, sir ? " Yes, we were ready, and off we went, down over the shell-shattered ground to the foot-bridge as fast as we could go, on to the bridge that was of every shape and level, for it had been blown up times without number, and repaired again by our engineers, who had more than half their men killed and wounded on the work of keeping the bridges in repair.

We did not tarry on the bridge, for shrapnel burst over us, a shell landed just behind us, and we scrambled up the opposite bank as quickly as possible. We met one of the water-carriers who had been caught by one of the shells, but was more scared than hurt, for his wound was slight. I said to him, " Well, you ought to thank God you have come out so well." " Indeed I do, indeed I do ! " said he. Up the road and over the fallen débris we went, out past " Suicide Corner," with shells falling before and behind (I can see them bursting on the farm-house where our artillery were posted, as I write, for these scenes are indelibly impressed on the memory). After a long walk we got out of range; then a staff car gave us a lift, and we got back to Ghyvelde, very tired, after a rather exhausting day.

I may explain a little the position at Nieuport : the enemy had already captured the Lombardzyde sector when we went up, the canal ran in front of Nieuport; we held the side of the canal on which Nieuport was situated, and the Redan, a triangular piece of ground, with some trenches on the other side. In this comparatively small area we had three battalions, most of them living in open trenches which were just possible in fine weather, and impossible in wet. The shelters on the Redan itself were just dug out of the earth, and the men were packed so tightly together that one had to clamber over their bodies in the darkness to make one's way round.

Shells rained down upon us from every side, of every size from 4·2 to huge 17-inch shells, that fell and burst giving forth a shock like that of an earthquake. The only access across the water was by three narrow floating bridges, named respectively Putney Bridge, Crowther Bridge, and Vauxhall Bridge; besides these, there was what was known as the " Five Bridges," the old stone bridge of the town, which ran in a sort of semicircle across the river and certain other streams, took one a long way round, and was under fire more or less all the time.

All our water had to be carried up day by day by the water-carriers across these bridges, so the water-carrier's task was by no means a pleasant one. Some humorist had chalked up a notice : *No loitering on the bridge,* and *Fishing from the bridges is strictly prohibited.* I never saw anyone give the least sign of loitering : a glance round, as one emerged from the tunnel, a dash over the shell-torn ground, on to the bridge with eyes fixed on the farther shore, across, and up the other bank and away ; a hundred yards from the bridge one could breathe again. The bridges are firmly imaged on the minds of all who have had to cross them and live in the Redan.

The town was a total wreck, shelled out of recognition ; a trench ran up the principal street, just sufficing to keep off shell fragments, that was all ; it was constantly getting blown in, and from it some other tunnels branched off and took one within 100 yards of the river bank.

On Sunday, July 29th, the troops were all busy practising the attack, I had a large number of Communions at night and said a few words before we went into action. Monday was spent in getting ready for the move. Tuesday we rose early ; I said Mass for the last time in Ghyvelde church, bade good-bye to the curé, a most excellent and devoted man, who was working most zealously, his church open all day, Exposition and Benediction of the Blessed Sacrament every night, at which there was always a good attendance, as well as at the early Mass.

The march was a long one, and we reached our

destination, Oost Dunkerque, about 1 o'clock, after a four hours' tramp. The day was overcast and rain was falling when we got in; I found I had to walk back to Coxyde Bains, so there was nothing to do but set off again. Our guns had been busy all the morning; as we turned our steps towards Coxyde enemy shells went singing over our heads. At a turn in the road I entered a shed to inquire the way; the man pointed out the spot where the shells were bursting: " That's the place you want, sir." We decided to wait till things quietened a little.

After a while the firing ceased, we went on, and found our billet was a fine new house, beautifully furnished, with good beds, and indeed everything that could be desired, and we wondered why no one else had taken it. We did not wonder long: we were sitting down to tea, when crash! at the front, crash! at the back, the sound of falling glass, crash! all round us; the enemy's heavy shells were falling on every side. The shower only lasted a short time, but was repeated every two hours until nearly midnight; after that we were troubled no more.

One day, walking through Coxyde, I said to the man on point duty, " Where is the Town Major ? " " Oh, at such a place." " He's moved ? " I said. " Oh, he—why, he's always a-moving; when the shells finds him he hops it," was the reply.

I said Mass in my room the two days we were here. Those days the rain never ceased the whole time. Our boys moved up in the darkness of that Thursday night, and were simply saturated long before they reached the trenches; happily they had few casualties, but the ceaseless rain and the flooded trenches made the first days very trying for all.

AT NIEUPORT

On Friday I went up to Nieuport to take over at the advanced dressing station, where I was to sleep during the time in the line. The station consisted of the lower part of a factory : the upper part had been entirely blown away by shell fire. There was one large chamber which was used for attending to the wounded, and orderly room, etc.; then out of it a series of narrow passages in which the R.A.M.C. men lived; at the end of it a small room used as the mess, with a small opening which let in the light of day. Another chamber opened off the reception room, with a brick barrel roof; in this the three doctors and myself used to sleep.

The day was even worse than the two preceding ones, the rain descending in a flood all the time. I got a lift on an ambulance car, which took me to a point half-way up; here I had to wait for another car by one of our 11-inch batteries. I found a number of Catholics who had been without the Sacraments for some time, so I was able to give them Holy Communion in the interval of waiting. The second car took me within 100 yards of the A.D.S.; Nieuport looked more utterly forlorn and desolate than ever in the heavy deluge of rain under which I saw it that morning. I completed my arrangements for moving in on the morrow, and returned drenched to the skin to Coxyde. The next day, Saturday, I moved into my new quarters in the A.D.S. The shelling was exceptionally heavy and the three bridges were all broken; all communication with the Redan was practically cut off.

Next morning I said Mass in an underground shelter, with just a few men assisting; the shells were crashing around us all the day and night without ceasing. The bridges were broken again almost as soon as repaired. On Monday I managed to get across Crowther Bridge, with great difficulty; the other two bridges were still broken. I made my way along the trenches and gave Holy Communion to the men of the 5th and 6th Battalions.

The day following, August 7th, we were unable to cross any of the footbridges, as the shelling was too heavy; however, we got round over the stone bridges, and thence on to the men of the 4th Battalion, who were on the right of the Redan. The shells fell very close all the while, and several times showers of fragments rattled down on us; then, in an interval of quiet, we made a dash across to the "Rubber House" and got a runner to go round the 5th Battalion. I was always glad I went that day, as several of our boys were killed in the terrible bombardment of the following night. The Holy Communion of that morning was their Viaticum.

I remember one of the men came back with me to the bridge and watched me cross, and never moved till he saw me safe on the other side; I turned and waved farewell to him with my stick. It was the last time I was to see him alive.

That night was one of the most terrible we experienced. The evening shelling was terrific and without respite. Shells rained down upon us from every side. The "Rubber House" certainly justified its name. Shells crashed and burst all around and over it, but not one of them pierced its walls. The whole of the headquarters servants, including the regimental sergeant-major and most of the office staff, were buried by our ammunition dump, which was exploded by one of the enemy shells and blew up, making an immense crater in the ground.

All through the night I was up with the wounded, who were streaming in from the Northumberland Fusiliers, who had made an attack on the right and suffered severely.

Our 6th Battalion had also raided and captured a few prisoners, with comparatively small losses; the 4th went up to try and hold the position, but were obliged to fall back.

Captain Weeks, who was in charge, set a wonderful example to all: no words can describe his unsparing devotion; never tired nor weary, he tended the terribly mangled men who poured in night and day; wonderfully skilful and amazingly gentle, he had the entire devotion of every man there, and they would have followed him anywhere. He was relieved the night before I was, and the men were discussing the change. " You don't expect to find another like him, do you ? " said one. And what higher praise can any officer receive than that ? I have seen him worn and strained, the shells crashing all around, attending the terribly battered victim on the table, doing all that a man could do to spare unnecessary pain; a fearful crash, the building quivered, the electric light was cut off and we were plunged in darkness. Just a quiet call for candles, and he went on calmly and undisturbed with his work. Every morning at 5 o'clock he went round and personally visited every one of the forward posts, with utter disregard of his own safety.

Thus the days passed by, never a moment's cessation from the ceaseless crash, and whenever we went to our mess the shells always began dropping outside more rapidly, and the pieces rattled against the wire netting we had put across the opening to stop their entry.

A new doctor came up and we had just sat down to dinner. It was his first experience under fire. The shells crashed on as usual, and the young doctor started at each crash. At last he exclaimed: " D—— that gun! Oh, I beg your pardon, Father, I really can't help it." Highly strung, yet brave, he went round the lines, and was delighted with the work, the hardship and discomfort of our life, for, said he, " It is what I came out for," and he was awfully disappointed when recalled.

Another man who won admiration up there was Captain Montgomery, a Canadian, who showed extraordinary courage on the terrible night when our headquarters staff were killed, and inspired with something of his own fearlessness all the R.A.M.C. boys who were with him in the post near the Rubber House. One of the elephant huts was blown up, and there was a call for volunteers to dig the buried men out. One of them was one of our Catholic boys, and he said to me: " Father, I just put my little crucifix in front of me, made my act of contrition, and asked our Lord to help me, and so, as I dug, I moved my crucifix forward till the work was complete."

At all hours of the day men crept up to me for Confession and Holy Communion, as I had told them that when I was not along the line I was always on duty at the dressing station. How many fervent Communions were made in the tunnels and the various corners of the dressing station during those days!

On Friday, August 18th, our men had succeeded in digging out the bodies of six of our men, and I went over the Redan to bury them. I have rarely seen anything quite so pathetic : the grave, dug in Flanders mud, was already filling with water; the poor bodies in their uniform as they had fallen, the utter desolation of everything all around made up a scene not easily forgotten. The adjutant and the burial party stood by; I had only just begun the burial office when a shell burst close by. "Don't make the service too long, Father," whispered my servant over my shoulder. Two or three more came over ere the ceremony was complete, and the burial party began hastily filling in the grave. "You had better get across as soon as you can," said the adjutant to me, after the ceremony was over; I again got across with nothing worse than some shrapnel bursting above me.

One night a party were crossing when the enemy dropped a shell on the bridge and the whole party were precipitated into the water; one poor fellow sank twice, and was going down the third time when he said within himself : " O God, if You'll only get me out of this, I will never be the same again." With that he clutched desperately at some weeds, and a hand caught hold of him and drew him to shore. He was still trembling and shaken from the shock when I saw him, and full of most fervent resolves as to his future life.

One day, coming back across the stone bridge, we had a narrow escape. It was difficult to tell how the shells were falling as we went along, and there was a party of about twenty of us straggling out in a long line, with myself and servant in the rear.

Suddenly a 5·9 shell burst at the side of the road; as the smoke cleared away we saw two of the foremost men on the ground. O'Grady and myself ran forward and helped to carry them into one of the ruined houses, where they were both quickly bandaged and placed upon the stretchers found near by. Luckily the succeeding shells fell farther away, or our whole party would have been knocked out. It was my first experience of carrying a wounded man; by the time we reached the A.D.S. I was pretty well exhausted, and realised what straining work stretcher-bearing is.

We had just sat down to breakfast one morning when a terrific convulsion shook the whole place. "That was not a 5·9, was it?" About twenty minutes passed, another earthquake-like shock, and so it went on the whole day every twenty minutes. We found later he was sending over 17-inch shells, as half of one of the base plates was picked up near by, and it was all one man could do to carry it.

I had to go round to brigade headquarters, waited till the shock had come, and then made a dash for it. I had just finished my business there and was thinking of trying to get back before the next shell came over, when a few men came flying down the cellar steps and a mighty crash at the side announced another arrival.

These visitors only ceased coming over about 7 o'clock, and when we had only 5·9s coming over we felt they were quite a pleasant sound. All the time our numbers were getting steadily reduced, for we were so crowded into the narrow salient of the Redan that such shelling as we had endured could not fail to claim many victims; and we began to wonder who would be left if we were not soon relieved. The strain on everyone was intense. Colonel Tew went down to bring up reinforcements, and he said to me: " When I got down there and looked at myself in the glass, I could not believe it was myself, my face was so haggard and worn." He came back just after the big shells had come over ; one of them had burst near the headquarters, and some of the curious had measured the hole— 40 feet in diameter and 19 feet deep. " Have you been to see the big hole, sir ? " said one of the young officers. " No," said he, " and I don't intend to, either."

I shall always remember the last day : we had been erecting some elephant huts and sandbagging them in a ruined house at the side of our dressing station ; it so happened the only outward and visible sign of what they were destined for was a pile of shells for the 18-pounders near by. An enemy plane flew over in the morning, and then a barrage was laid down and 9·2 shells rained upon us the entire day. It was the most trying day of all. We had been arguing as to whether the shells were 5·9 or 9·2, when suddenly with a crash a complete baseplate from one of the shells fell at our feet and decided the argument in favour of 9·2.

The whole place was quivering and shaking with the shock of bursting shells, our building was struck in all directions, many direct hits, and yet never a shell came through. All through the day boys came up to me in the semi-darkness : " Will you hear my confession, Father, and give me Holy Communion ? " Nearly everyone was feeling we could not come through, yet I felt so confident that I lay down and had a good hour's sleep in the afternoon, and about 8 o'clock the bombardment ceased. There had been many casualties around us, but not one amongst those at the dressing station.

One morning there was a Canadian officer on duty, a most excellent man with a high sense of duty, and a devout Presbyterian. A poor fellow came in who had been blown up by a shell, very shaken and scared, but not injured, when the following dialogue ensued: " Well, my man, blown up? Were you completely buried?" " No, sir, not quite, but I was stuck in; they had to dig me out." " What are you, conscript or soldier?" " Soldier, sir." " Well, I suppose you know soldiers are liable to be killed, don't you?" " Yes, sir." " Well, then, take a few of these "—handing him some tablets—" pray over it and you'll be all right."

On the last morning, just as our bearers were crossing the stone bridge, they were caught by a shell: two were killed and others injured. One of them, J. Byrne, was a Catholic. His body was brought in on a stretcher, and I offered the Holy Sacrifice for him, with his body lying near by the temporary altar. Most of the boys came to assist, and all the Catholics offered their Holy Communion for him.

At last, on Thursday, August 16th, the news came that we were to be relieved the next night. The relief, a very difficult operation, began at 9 o'clock in the evening and was completed by 3 o'clock the next morning, Friday, August 17th. I waited on till the last of our boys had passed through, and then, as the sun was coming up, I got on the lorry that was waiting and went along the road to Coxyde. The sunrise, one of the most glorious I have ever seen, seemed to harmonise well with our own feelings, and, as the colonel remarked, nature rejoiced with us at our deliverance.

I cannot describe the feeling of relief at being able to walk about freely in the sunshine after our underground life and ceaseless watching against shells whenever above ground. It was like returning from death to life, as indeed we all felt it was.

As soon as I reached our quarters at Coxyde I procured a bath, and I remember, as I was looking over my underclothing to rid myself of undesirable visitors, Major Walker looked in: " Hullo, the Padre at his daily task," he remarked on seeing the work on which I was engaged.

The whole division, or rather the survivors of it, was utterly exhausted by the tremendous strain through which we had passed, and so we were sent to La Panne, a delightful seaside resort where the King of the Belgians had his residence, and where the troops were to recuperate. It was like coming from hell to heaven.

We marched out from the camp at Coxyde and reached La Panne in the afternoon, and just as we came in a few shells sang over the dunes in the distance, reminders of what we had been through.

CHAPTER V

QUIET DAYS AT LA PANNE

ON Saturday morning I walked back to Coxyde and then on to Oost Dunkerque. As I was going along I observed five planes flying fairly low, which I took to be ours; however, I learnt, on reaching Oost Dunkerque, that they were enemy planes, and had just been bombing; one of the Australian gunners had been killed outright and another very badly wounded.

We found a beautiful modern Gothic church, with a very bright and cheerful interior, where we had Mass and Benediction for the troops weekdays and Sundays. It was served by the Oblates of Mary Immaculate, whose convent was beside the church. The troops greatly appreciated the opportunities afforded them in this sanctuary, after all we had been through in the line. I spoke strongly on the importance of being grateful to God for their deliverance, and the necessity of avoiding excess in drink after the strain of the line. It so happened that, in spite of my exhortations, one or two cases of drunkenness occurred, so next Sunday morning I said, " Greatly as I regret it, I think it well to make a rule that no man shall drink more than two pints of beer a day, which I think is ample for anyone." A few days after one of our soldiers met me and said : " Well, Father, I've always been a teetotaller, but since you told us we *must* drink two pints of beer a day, I've been doing it." Which shows how easily one's best-intentioned efforts can be misconstrued.

The officers of the battalion were quartered in an hotel on the sea front, and all the troops in the town were very comfortably billeted, and spirits soon revived in the pleasant surroundings, with sea-bathing and all the pleasures of a seaside town. The townsfolk were kindly and hospitable, and with the splendid weather gave a delightful sense of homeliness and tranquillity.

The town had never been either bombed or shelled, and except for a certain amount of inevitable neglect owing to want of sufficient labour, retained its peace-time aspect.

Owing to the way various units were spread out, I still had to go over to Coxyde and Oost Dunkerque and arrange for the spiritual needs of the troops there.

Until August 30th nothing occurred to disturb our peaceful tranquillity; that morning was rather overcast, with the clouds rather low. The trench mortar battery had just moved in, as they had remained back in the line for some time after we came out. I had just got out the words : " This is a delightful place; it is never shelled or bombed," when crash, crash, crash! came from first one side of the house and then another. " Well, what's that, then ? " exclaimed the captain. We went to the door and found a German plane had been over and dropped a number of bombs on the town. I went out to see what had happened; at the corner of the road the military policeman I had been speaking to only a few minutes before had been instantly killed by one of the bombs; another had fallen beside the church and blown in most of the windows. It was the first bombing attack, but by no means the last. The children were struggling in the holes blown by the bombs, to gather fragments as souvenirs, almost as soon as they had fallen, for it was a new experience for them, and as yet they had not learned by experience the deadly nature of the bomb whose relics they were so eagerly collecting. Every night we stood and watched the German bombing planes going over to their destructive work at Dunkerque, and the great fires caused by them there shone brightly across the sea coast on those fine September nights. Bright flashes of bursting shrapnel followed the enemy planes, who evaded the search-lights very cleverly, very few being caught in their rays compared to the number that passed over night by night.

Our transport officer had been on leave, and on the day he returned (September 5th) our mess went to the cinema on the front. It was poorly housed in a half-finished hotel and a very ordinary affair, with a small band of Belgian musicians, but a great attraction to the troops. That night it was "Officers only," and the room was packed with well over 200 officers from the various units in the town. All went well until about the middle of the performance, when a terrific crash near by, quickly followed by two others, the last sending showers of broken brickwork against the side of the building, gave unmistakable evidence that enemy planes were over us. The band played on and everyone remained quietly in their places as if nothing had happened; luckily the next three bombs fell well away. When we came out we found the sentry had been killed instantly, his head severed from his body by a fragment of one of the bombs, a number of houses demolished, the windows of our hotel blown in, and a number of civilians and soldiers wounded.

When we got to our mess the next morning we found how very nearly we had been to being caught the previous night. In the very place where each night we used to stand watching the planes go over was the hole made by a bomb. If it had not been for our going to the cinema that night the bomb would have landed on top of our little group, and swiftly ended our days here below.

Father Gordon, a most devoted priest, was killed by a shell in his billet in Coxyde during this week, and there was a large and representative attendance at the solemn requiem Mass in the parish church on Thursday morning. Most of the Catholic army chaplains in the neighbourhood, and representatives from various denominations, several Belgian generals and a number of British staff officers attended to pay homage to the memory of a brave and devoted priest.

On Saturday, September 1st, the Divisional General held an inspection of our brigade on the shore and distributed a number of medals to officers and men gained during the operations at Nieuport. Just as the troops were marching off the enemy landed his first shell in the town. It entered the hospital store and wrecked it entirely: I have rarely seen a more complete piece of work. This was followed by a number of other shells on succeeding days, naturally causing a certain amount of anxiety to the townsfolk.

The weeks passed very quickly and pleasantly, and, like all good things, our stay drew to a close. Towards the end of our time at La Panne, Colonel Tew left us and was succeeded by Colonel Walker. The intended operations before Nieuport were finally abandoned, as all military opinion became more and more averse to the project. However, the first hint we had of the change was the movement of our heavy guns away in the direction of Ypres, for we were still expecting the attack to be pressed. All sorts of rumours were abroad during the last days: we were going back to Nieuport, we were going down to Lavantie, we were going south, we were going to Ypres; and this last rumour proved true.

The work during these days was very absorbing and interesting, as the whole country between La Panne and the front line was filled with artillery of every conceivable kind, in fact the sand-dunes simply bristled with guns, many of which never fired a shot. We were all disappointed at the abandonment of the project, although it was evident enough that we could only hope for success, if attained at all, at an enormous sacrifice of life.

Besides artillery and engineers, there was a number of labour companies working along the roads, and many men in these units had not approached the Sacraments for years, so when I came along I was gratefully welcomed. The men would step off the road into the field at the side, kneel down, make their confession and then receive Holy Communion. I shall always remember their gratitude, and the "Thank you, Father," "God bless you, Father, and keep you safe," uttered with such intense sincerity, repaid one a thousand times for the long tramps under the hot sun along dusty roads, for the roads of Flanders are either extremely dusty or else quagmires of mud.

On our last Sunday in La Panne the King of the Belgians came out of the church just as our troops were drawn up to enter for their Mass; they gave the salute as he passed along us to his house on the right of the church. We left La Panne with regret and carried away from it many happy memories, the kindness of the people and religious in charge of the church, who freely placed it at our disposal for the spiritual needs of the boys.

On Thursday, September 19th, we set out on our march back to Bray Dunes, which we reached about midday; here we spent a few days preparatory to moving down to the south of St. Omer for three weeks' training.

We began our march on Sunday, September 23rd : the day was beautifully fine ; the sea and the sand-dunes soon left behind ; and we reached Teteghem in the early afternoon.

I assisted at Vespers and Benediction in the beautiful old village church. Within the church that quiet Sunday afternoon the scene was supremely peaceful, and characteristic of the worship in the small country villages of France. A large congregation, of old and young, four singing boys in scarlet and white, and the curé, with one old singing man, just dimly seen through the haze of incense, a striking contrast to the distant rumble of the guns from without. The service was rendered with reverent care, and the whole congregation joined heartily in singing the Psalms and Canticles.

I had to rise very early to say Mass next morning, to be ready for our long march to Warmhoudt. The day was hot, and by the time we drew near the town our men were very tired ; but they freshened up as the great spire of the church came in sight, and marched in with a fine swing. The people lined the streets and roads to welcome us in, as the rumour of our coming had reached them through our billeting party; the regiment had been there before and was very popular in the town.

The church was a glorious structure of the early sixteenth century, with a magnificent tower and spire and noble and dignified interior. I stayed the night at the presbytery and was most heartily welcomed by the parish clergy.

Unfortunately our stay was only for one night, and I was just able to say Mass by rising early, as we were on the move again by 7 o'clock next morning. The day was fine and very hot, the march a long one, and we reached our destination feeling pretty tired after it all. Our billets were scattered about a great deal in various farm-houses, so that the brigade was spread out over a wide area. The church at Buysscheure was exceedingly well kept, and I found the curé a most charming personality, one of the finest priests I have met in France. He was devoted to his work and his people, and they in turn were devoted to him.

On the next day he was having Exposition of the Blessed Sacrament all day, and he invited me to dine with a number of other priests who were coming in for the occasion. The whole countryside ceased work for that day and spent it in church. Great numbers received Holy Communion all the early hours of the morning, and at the solemn Mass of Exposition at 11 o'clock the church was packed to overflowing. The earnestness and devotion of the congregation, the reverent behaviour of the little acolytes, all evidenced the fruit of the curé's devoted work.

The dinner was an interesting occasion, and showed

that the curé was as loved and popular amongst his clerical brethren as amongst his own people, and the conversation naturally turned a great deal on England and the position of the Catholic Church there. Solemn Vespers and Benediction in the afternoon brought the great day to a close.

After two days' rest we set out on our way, once more starting very early in the morning. As we were standing at the cross-roads I heard a voice say, " Our billet is on fire." I turned and looked across towards the farm-house we had just left, and saw great volumes of smoke issuing from the barn on one side of the quadrangle; a company of men were immediately sent back to render aid, but in spite of all their efforts three sides of the building were destroyed in an extremely short space of time.

Our march was a very long one, and after we had passed through St. Omer we halted in a large field for lunch. It was glorious weather, and officers and men alike enjoyed this picnic in the open immensely.

We reached our destination, Esquerdes, a charming old-world village, with a most interesting twelfth-century country church (just recently declared a public monument, as the curé informed me), about half-past four in the afternoon. The surroundings were delightful; we were all exceedingly well billeted, warmly welcomed by the people, and were looking forward to a very pleasant three weeks' stay while we were doing our training; but, alas for the mutability of all human things, we had hardly sat down to dinner when we heard we were to leave and march with all haste to Ypres.

A day's rest, and just a little time to study the intensely interesting church, with its fine central tower and spire, and to become a little acquainted with the beautiful country around, and again we were on the move.

CHAPTER VI

THE STRUGGLE FOR PASSCHENDAELE

A LONG march past Cassell brought us to a village north of Hazebrouck. It was rather small and billets hard to find, but at last, after a good deal of difficulty, a good woman arranged a room for myself with a small place for my servant, and did everything in her power for our comfort, full of apology that she could not do more. Her son was far away on the French battle front, and she was only too eager to do anything for our fighting men, and especially pleased that she was able to provide shelter for a priest.

The church here was a very fine spacious structure in Early Gothic style, and well kept.

The enemy bombing machines were busy the whole night long and came over in relays bombing the whole country very heavily, especially Hazebrouck and Cassell. Next morning I walked into Hazebrouck, as I heard my old confrère Father Charles Murphy was there with the Australian troops on the way up to Passchendaele. We had been trying to meet for days, and the distance between us in time and space had grown steadily less; and here I found the troops had left only seven hours before. The enemy's bombing machines were constantly over during my walk, and fragments of shrapnel fell pretty close on my way back from Hazebrouck.

On October 2nd we set out for our camp in the Watou area, and reached it after a trying march, just as night was falling. The tents were very crowded, but we all managed to get under cover in some way or another as the night was cold and frosty.

Just as we were going off to sleep, the news came through that some of us must go back to Watou to attend the court of inquiry into the burning of our farm billet at Broxelle. The intelligence officer, the second in command, myself and some other ranks were called back on this unimportant matter at the very moment we were moving up to battle; but such is the way in the Army, typical of the methodical order in which everything is dealt with.

As the troops moved off towards Red Rose Camp we set out for Watou, which we reached only to find we were expected to stay the night and go back to Buysscheure, where the court of inquiry was to be held the day following. As I had arranged to give general Communion to our men that afternoon, I went back to Red Rose Camp, while the others decided to await my return in the evening. By jumping lorries I managed to get as far as Poperinghe, and then got another lift along the fine road that runs thence to Vlamertinghe and Ypres. I reached Red Rose Camp and explained the situation to Colonel Walker; he was furious, as the second in command had all the arrangements for the attack in hand. Ultimately, after much wiring and 'phoning, one of the officers came back with the papers. As soon as I arrived I set to work with all speed to get our men together for the general Communion.

The day was raw and cold, and General Lewis, with the kindness and thoughtfulness so characteristic of him, had the large hut he was using cleared and a table prepared for Holy Communion, so that the troops might all shelter inside. Night was coming on when all had assembled. The shed was packed,

and the congregation sang the Benediction service
and some of the favourite hymns with great fervour.
I spoke a few words, exhorting them to entire confidence in Almighty God and entire conformity to
His Holy Will, whatever that will might be, and then
Holy Communion followed. So great was the pack
that the men could not move up, so I had to make my
way line by line and fracture the hosts several times
that all might be able to receive. That for some
was the last time I was to see them alive, and there
was a great sense of solemnity over us all, as we knew
how desperate was the struggle into which we were
going; so that the hymn after Holy Communion,
" Soul of my Saviour," was singularly appropriate.
The moment of silence while the blessing of Our
Lord was bestowed was only broken by the half-
suppressed sobs of some of the younger boys. All
pressed round me as we went out, to express their
grateful gladness at being able to be strengthened
for the conflict by the Bread of the strong.

I was distressed at not going up with them, but I
had immediately to turn back to Watou, and by
means of changing from one lorry to another I got
back to my destination, where I spent the night at
the house of the curé.

I said Mass in the stately old church at 6.30, and at
that early hour the church was filled with a large
congregation and line after line of communicants
were kneeling at the altar rails.

A motor bus, one of the old London road cars,
took us on our way and we arrived at Buysscheure
numbed with cold. The court of inquiry was to sit
in one of the larger houses of the village, and the
whole family from the farm-house was there in a state

of tears and emotion, with an old lawyer who was advising them. One by one the witnesses went in, and then an amusing interlude occurred between the lawyer and the divisional interpreter. The lawyer asserted that the interpreter was not faithfully translating the evidence of his witnesses; the interpreter, whose very mobile face showed every passing emotion, laid his hand on his heart and called Heaven to witness that he had truthfully translated every word. The dialogue and the dramatic action of the two gave a relief to a very tiring time; however, at last all the evidence was taken and the court finally broke up.

We got on our bus once more, and arrived back at Red Rose Camp late in the evening half frozen, to find the battalion had already gone up; but the transport had not moved, so we had a tent to sleep in and some food to restore warmth to our bodies.

The next morning, Friday, October 5th, I went up to Wieltje, where in a deep dugout the advanced dressing station was established.

We went through Ypres, past the prison, on through its ruined streets to St. Jean, now only a heap of broken brickwork and masonry, the whole countryside scarred and blasted by shell fire, trees and all verdure destroyed, the roads a quagmire of mud, crammed with transport, men, and guns all pressing forward. I went down into the underground passages where the brigade headquarters were established. The water was only kept down by ceaseless pumping, and the whole atmosphere was moist, heavy, and oppressive, and most of the staff were suffering badly from headache; only a few candles cast an uncertain light in these catacombs. The tunnels linked us up with the dressing station, where accommodation was extremely bad, so that I had to return to Dead End at Ypres to sleep at night. The weather was wretchedly wet and cold, and I was utterly worn out and hungry when I stumbled on some engineers who had their quarters in the ramparts.

They gave me a hearty welcome to their mess, and we spent an enjoyable evening, and for the moment forgot the discomfort without. I made my way forward through the mud—real Ypres mud (those who have been there will know what I mean), to the headquarters of the ambulance: here I obtained a stretcher and rolled myself in some blankets and succeeded in getting warm enough to sleep. I rose early the next morning and set out once more along the road out through St. Jean, where I met Watt, the Presbyterian padre, and we went on to Wieltje Farm. The rain poured down pitilessly: we were soon drenched to the skin, and our field boots gradually filled to the top with water. When we got to the station we found a number of dead bodies awaiting burial, but no burial party. I went down to brigade; they rang up the divisional burial officer, and the only change we got out of him was, he would come and inspect the bodies to-morrow. " We don't want the bodies inspected, but buried," said I. " Well, we will have another try." And we set out in the driving rain once more. At last, in a very poor little dugout, just a few sheets of corrugated iron to keep the worst of the rain off, we found some officers, and I asked them if they would have the charity to give us a few men to dig a grave and form a burial party. The senior officer very kindly arranged the matter at once, and a sergeant and six men were detailed to do the work. While the men dug we both set to work, searched the bodies for such evidence as we could find as to the identity of each one, then prepared rough crosses to mark the place each one occupied. The men dug with a will and the grave was soon made ready, and each of the bodies was gently placed in position in the grave. I said the service for the Catholics and Padre Watt for the others, and then we stood by till the grave was filled in. The rain came down without a moment's respite, and the men who had performed this work of charity were soon as wet as ourselves. I thanked them most fervently for what they had done, and then they made their way back to their comfortless shelter, where they were awaiting orders to move forward.

We passed on up the road, with its press of moving limbers, guns, pack animals, and men all pressing relentlessly forward like a great machine. Piled up on either side of the road or trampled underfoot were the carcasses of decaying mules and horses, streaking the mud with red, the bodies of men, slain as they went up, smashed and overturned limbers, and all the wreckage that marked the roads of the Ypres sector, shells occasionally bursting in the desolate, war-torn country on either side, the unceasing song of shells passing overhead; by the roadside at one point lay horse and rider, just as they had fallen the night before, half buried in the mud and slime, trampled down by the ceaseless forward movement that never seemed to stay by day or night. Such was the road to the front line. Well forward in one of the concrete pill-boxes on the left of the road we found our machine gunners. To effect an entry was not easy, as one had to drop down a narrow area and then slide backwards down a still narrower opening and so into the interior. Here officers and men were simply packed together in this underground chamber, filled with steam arising from their saturated clothing.

I gave Holy Communion to our boys, and Padre Watt spoke a few words to the others, and after a short rest we clambered out once more into the open.

We next made our way to the line of little concrete pill-boxes where our trench mortar battery was established, and received the warm welcome from them which we always found waiting whenever we visited them, no matter what the circumstances.

They provided tea for us somehow, in spite of all the difficulty of getting provisions up; it was indeed welcome.

In one of these small pill-boxes, as they were well named, our Catholic boys assembled. The building was so low that we could not stand upright. By the light of a solitary candle, all crouching down, we sang " Faith of Our Fathers," " Sweet Sacrament Divine," and " Soul of My Saviour," and then after Benediction all the boys received Holy Communion. Shorn of every outward sign of solemnity, yet I scarcely remember a service more impressive than this, in that cramped underground vault, with the voices of the singers within punctuated with the crash of shells without.

Night was falling as we moved back towards Ypres. From the shells came forth great flashes of light as they burst on either side of us as we went. Darkness had fallen long before I reached Ypres, where I spent the night on the ramparts with the field ambulance.

Monday morning I went up to St. Jean, where I met Padre Watt again, and we both set out along the road to the forward lines; rain was falling slightly; the heaviness of the day matched the unutterably desolate surroundings through which we had to pass. We followed the road with its pack of men, limbers, and animals crushed together and pressing ever onward. After a while we came on the road formed by great teak planks of timber, the only way it was possible to form a way through the liquid mud. The way was slippery and uncertain as the planks were covered with slush and mud, and spaces between made pitfalls for the unwary.

After a while we left the road and struck off along the duckboard track that led to the forward lines. As we advanced every sign of vegetation ceased; long gaunt poles that had once been trees indicated the place where little woods had formerly stood; not even a blade of grass relieved the utter desolation. The whole ground as far as the eye could reach was just brown earth ploughed up by countless thousands of shells. For shell-hole broke into shell-hole whichever way one looked. Woe to those who forsook the duckboards or the white tape lines, for once away from these all sense of location was lost, and many a man returning from the line had fallen down in helpless despair to die in a shell crater when almost within reach of succour.

We found brigade headquarters just a series of dugouts covered with brown earth, broken bricks and rubbish, a great bump out of the ground that one only recognised when close to it.

The General readily improvised a meal for us, and after a short stay we set out along the track once more. Shells began to fall unpleasantly close, but we kept on our way. At one point we met some of the 4th Battalion carrying some of the boys who had just been knocked out ; a little farther, and the dead body of one of the party lay beside the duckboards, where he had fallen a few minutes before, face and body smothered in blood.

The shelling increased as we went, and the black bursts were casting up mud and fragments all along the route. I was a little in front of Padre Watt. I heard his voice : " Get down ! " coming from behind me, and turning, saw him dropping into a shell-hole. Crash! came the shell in front of me as I followed his example, and the pieces rattled down. So we made our way forward, alternately walking along the duckboards and dropping into shell-holes to avoid the nearer bursts.

The duckboards ended, and we were descending into the valley, when an officer met us : " What are you doing here ? " " We are looking for the 5th Battalion headquarters." " You have passed them : they are right behind you on the sky-line there."

We turned back and approached one of the bumps which rose out of the universal brownness, and as we approached we found men lying on stretchers all around, and some of the less seriously wounded sheltering themselves as best they could from the enemy fire under the rubbish heap beneath which the regimental aid post was situated. Inside it was a crush of wounded men, and stretcher-bearers resting from their task. The doctor was working as hard as he could seeing to the worst cases, while those who could walk were sent back along the duckboards to the dressing station down at Wieltje Farm. After a few minutes here we made a dash in the direction of some other bumps in the ground, and one of them proved to be the headquarters. Officers, clerks, and runners were all packed together in the small concrete dugout, whose most vulnerable side faced the foe. The second in command, as the shells came crashing without, told us quite cheerfully : " They will put a shell through us soon."

The barrage remained very heavy, and Colonel Walker asked us to wait till things were a little quieter. As soon as we could we set out again ; along the top of the ridge lay a row of tanks knocked out by the enemy's anti-tank guns, and beside one a dead soldier was still standing upright. Everywhere we passed the bodies of the slain lying in the shell-holes, and the flesh of one Highlander was already falling from his bones, for this gun-swept area was such that no risks could be taken, and burial parties would have only sacrificed the living for the sake of the dead.

We met a large contingent of New Zealanders working, putting in the foundation for the timber track we were constructing. I called out to them : " Any Catholics here—step aside and you can have Absolution and Holy Communion." As it happened there was a considerable number, and as the news spread along the way, little groups fell out at the wayside to await me as I came along.

The dreary autumn day with its lowering clouds and mist of rain was closing in, the mass of shell-holes stretched out to the horizon, with here and there a few seared tree-trunks with every bough shot away, as the New Zealanders in little groups received Our Lord Who had come to them so unexpectedly in that place, and their gratitude was intensely moving. All around shells were falling and red flashes of light shone out from the black clouds of smoke and dust which they were casting up.

We more than once lost our direction, going back in endeavouring to reach the duckboard track, and the inky darkness had closed all from sight ere we reached Wieltje dressing station, and thence on through St. Jean once more back again to the ramparts at Ypres. The next day I spent at the dressing station, as wounded were coming down in a steady stream all day.

Father Guinness worked indefatigably for the next two nights and days above ground, never relaxing for a moment from his work with the walking wounded, giving them both spiritual and temporal consolation as they passed down.

The scene below, the improvised tables for tending the wounded in the narrow passages that formed the only sort of operating theatre possible, with the uncertain light, and the poor blood- and mud-stained victims, as they were borne in, was strangely fantastic, almost uncanny. The clothes had to be simply cut off in order to get at the terrible wounds, mostly inflicted by shell fire. Strange to say, one of the first officers to be borne down was the one who had come to our aid with the burial party a day or two before. The American doctor, who was just having his first experience of war, was bending over one of our wounded boys : " Ah, my poor man, you are badly hurt," said he. " Well, sir," was the response, " it's in a righteous cause." " Well," said the doctor, " let's hope it is. I don't think any cause can justify this."

So through those two long days and nights the men poured in from the most terrible fighting of the war. The difficulties of getting the wounded down added to the horror of those awful nights. Bearers heard voices calling to them out of the darkness, but dare not leave the duckboard tracks, for once they left these they were hopelessly lost, and added to this the enemy had all the tracks marked and was constantly dropping shells on to them, sending the duckboards up in the air, so that as men came along in the dark they fell headlong into the new-blown shell craters, and were lucky if on recovery they were able to find their bearings again.

Our brigade made their attack in the early hours of October 10th, and suffered heavy casualties, as did all the troops engaged during these fateful days.

Throughout the day and night of October 10th and 11th the labours of the doctors never ceased. Our troops came back very early on the morning of the 11th, and in the early hours of that morning the stream of sufferers began to slacken. About 7 o'clock I went up and found Father Guinness still at work, although utterly worn out and exhausted from want of food and sleep. I persuaded him at last to go down and promised I would follow two hours later, so as to be sure none of our wounded who might yet come down and need the Sacraments should be missed. During the night of the 10th and 11th Father Charles Murphy was badly wounded only a short distance away, but I heard nothing of it, as communication was so difficult, until several days later. The Australian losses had been terrible—far exceeding ours, and if a regiment only lost 60 per cent. of its number it was reckoned as light casualties.

The heroism of the men who fought for the Passchendaele heights can never be forgotten as long as human hearts remain to be moved by the story of magnificent and splendid sacrifice such as theirs. Lying in the drenching rain for hours, waiting for the moment to move forward to the assault, scarcely able to feel their rifles because numbed with cold; when the order came these men went on amidst the hail of shell fire of every conceivable kind, while the enemy machine guns, posted in the pill-boxes, were so placed as to cover the front with wonderful skill, and swept it with a relentless rain of fire.

Men stumbled forward in the uncertain light, falling in shell craters, struggling up again, ever pressing forward, their numbers thinning as they went, till only a handful reached the enemy lines; but they swept forward all the same, and although all the objectives were not taken, they did all that men could do that day.

And the uncomplaining spirit of the poor broken men who came back, mere masses of blood and mud, as they appeared in the dawning light of day: " Oh, I'm not so bad; see to Joe, he's worse hit than me; I can wait." Their grateful " Thank you " for any little help or the drink of hot cocoa we gave to all it was safe to do so; their courage and fortitude; their splendid endurance of pain and suffering—these have left an example of sublime self-sacrifice for all that come after.

At 9 o'clock I left the dressing station and made my way to X Camp a little way past St. Jean.

The men who survived were so utterly exhausted that they lay down in that field of mud and slept, regardless of everything. By the time I got down tents were being erected and shelters of all sorts dug in every direction. Alas, how many never came back. Many of the men, once they got their boots off, were unable to put them on again, and walked about in the mud with just a sandbag tied to each foot.

I went down on a lorry to Poperinghe, got a wash and shave, and when I went into the dining-room and looked round I found it hard to believe that what I saw was real.

The tables set with white tablecloths, cutlery, and glasses—such things seemed scarcely possible so short a distance behind the line, and yet so great a contrast. After lunch I went back again to X Camp, which everyone will remember. The enemy sent his shells over by day and bombed us by night.

One night, as we were having dinner in our tent, the hum of enemy planes sounded overhead, then there was a terrific crash at the side, our only candle was blown out, we were plunged in darkness, while great clods of earth and bits of timber rained down on our tent, wonderful to relate, without breaking it down. A moment later, and I heard Colonel Walker's voice outside, exclaiming, "Anyone hurt, anyone hurt?" "No, we are all right, sir." It was a marvellous escape and we were grateful for it.

We remained in reserve in this comfortless spot in the mud and the rain, glad to have a tent to cover us, for five days, and then the order came to move back to one of the camps in the Vlamertinghe area.

As we were marching through Ypres, I caught sight of one of the boys of the Australian troops to which Father Charles Murphy was attached, and learned for the first time that he was wounded.

As soon as we moved in to our new camp, a series of huts constructed of iron and wood, I jumped a lorry and made for the four clearing stations at Remi siding, but no trace of his having passed through could be found. I went back to Ypres, tried the various dressing stations there, then on to the divisional headquarters—all in vain.

On Wednesday I went down to see Father Bradley at Etaples. I was fortunate in getting a lorry as far as Abeele; there, after waiting some time, I picked up an Australian lorry which took me on as far as St. Omer. The driver told me Father Charles Murphy had died from wounds at a dressing station, and it was over a week before we heard otherwise.

At St. Omer the R.T.O. was extremely kind, and all who have been there have not hesitated to count him the very best and most helpful R.T.O. in France. He arranged tea and fixed me up on an ambulance train going down to the Base. The doctor in charge of the train was awfully kind, and provided an excellent dinner. I arrived at Etaples about 7 o'clock, and soon found my way to the I.B.D. where Father Bradley was located. It was our first meeting since the war began, and it was late ere we retired to rest. The next day we discussed the future a good deal, and I promised to do all I could to hasten arrangements for him to come up to the line.

On November 19th I travelled back to our camp, which I reached about 7.30 in the evening. We had only spent a short time in this camp, when orders came for us to proceed to Winnezeele on Wednesday morning. On that day I went to the conference of Catholic chaplains at Locre, to meet Cardinal Bourne, who was there making his visitation of the Western Front. After the conference we all went to the grave of Major Willie Redmond near by and recited together the *De Profundis*.

A long journey north, by means of lorry, the latter part on foot, brought us to our camp at Winnezeele, where after wandering about in the darkness I at last found our billet in a farm-house, where the people received us with great kindness and hospitality.

We remained a day there and then moved into Steenvoorde, where we spent some very happy days.

The troops began recuperating very quickly, and reinforcements soon helped to fill up the gaps the struggle at Passchendaele had made in our ranks.

CHAPTER VII

ON THE MENIN ROAD

THE church at Steenvoorde was a splendid specimen of sixteenth-century Gothic work, with a magnificently proportioned western tower that dominated the landscape for miles around, while the interior was spacious and finely proportioned. It was an immense consolation to be able to say our daily Mass in such a well-appointed church.

The curé was a man of exceptional force of character and ability, an eloquent preacher, and exercised a wonderful influence over the whole population.

I shall always remember the All Saints' festival there.

Six priests heard confessions throughout the eve of the festival from 6 o'clock in the morning till nearly 10 at night. Well over five hundred people received Holy Communion at the 7 o'clock Mass alone, and Masses were said from soon after 5 until the solemn High Mass at 10 o'clock. At the latter service the great church was packed to the doors with one of the most devout congregations I have ever seen, and again in the afternoon the church was packed for Vespers and Benediction.

We had nearly a fortnight in these peaceful surroundings; only heard the sound of gunfire far away, and bombing raids were few and far between.

The men much appreciated this church with its ever-open doors and continual round of services as well on weekdays as Sundays; in addition to the daily Masses, there was Benediction every night, at which large congregations always assisted.

The people of Steenvoorde were extremely friendly and sympathetic; always ready to do anything to make our stay as pleasant as possible.

The *suisse* of the church, a fine old man with a flowing white beard, himself an old soldier, found me a billet at the house of his daughter. Her two little boys were both altar servers, and most exemplary ones, too.

Just before the end of the time Colonel Walker gave a dinner on the occasion of his formal appointment as commander of the battalion. We passed a very happy evening together, and three days later we moved away to a camp at Dickebusch. The camp consisted of various kinds of hutments and a few half-ruined farm buildings. The whole country was more or less under mud and water, and rain descended incessantly. The brigade was much spread out, and on Saturday I made an effort to get in touch with everybody, but it was not easy work. I found all the units except the 4th, who were somewhere near Ypres. I walked across interminable tracks and roads, and as the afternoon advanced I witnessed quite a strange phenomenon. A black cloud rose from Ypres, gradually overspreading the whole heavens. Before I could get anywhere near home I was swallowed up in the inky blackness. I followed a track without the least idea of where I was going; after hours of wandering finally struck the right road and got home to our quarters at last, and found one of our officers had been lost in the same darkness for hours while going only a comparatively short distance.

On Sunday the trench mortars arranged their large hut for service and erected an excellent altar out of some cases of ammunition—certainly strange material out of which to construct it. The men attended in large numbers and received Holy Communion with great devotion, neither were we in any way disturbed by the air raid which accompanied our service.

On Monday morning we left for our new camp near Café Belge. The enemy shelled our camp almost as soon as we left it, and as we marched through the ruins of Dickebusch we could hear the shells crashing behind us.

Some of our battalions were situated in Swan Camp, which was well named, for it was more like a lake than anything else, with the huts sticking up out of the water. We were better off here for Holy Communion, as we were always able to get one of the huts in which the men could assemble. We had pretty heavy shelling most of the time here, but few casualties.

The walks these days were very interesting, stretching right up to Shrapnel Corner and Ypres, and out along the Warrington Road up to Halfway House brigade headquarters, placed appropriately enough between Hell Fire Corner and Hell Blast Corner, so, as the staff captain said, you can guess what our place is like. Those who were along the Menin Road in those days will fully appreciate the force of his remark.

The 7th Battalion were in dugouts, etc., on the side of the great plank road that ran from Shrapnel Corner right across to Halfway House and beyond.

In these days I realised more than ever the immense value of always carrying the Blessed Sacrament, for I came across all sorts of units—engineers, artillery, labour companies working on the roads; and everywhere was heartily welcomed by all and the opportunity of confession and Holy Communion gladly accepted.

The labour companies in this area were constantly under shell fire, entirely apart from the nightly bombing raids which were one unpleasant feature of our life in the salient. The whole area was swept by the enemy guns, and you never knew as you walked along when he would suddenly open out. The labour men working on the roads had a rough time, as they had no shelters to make for when the enemy laid down a barrage, and their only chance lay in scattering widely. The officers and N.C.O.s were always ready to do what they could, and willingly let the men off work for a short interval to receive the Sacraments; often they would go round and get our men together for me.

Many of the men on this work had not had the chance of hearing Mass for months, for the making of roads and ways up to the line permitted no rest from their labours.

Just as I was finishing my round near the Lille Gate one of our old boys from St. Gregory's came up to me: "Can you hear my confession, Father?" "Yes, and give you Holy Communion as well." He stepped on to the roadside for a few minutes, and went on his way immensely consoled, as he had not been able to receive Holy Communion for some time; indeed, in these strenuous days of ceaseless struggle and movement, this was the only way to enable the men to approach the Sacraments.

I saw Major Duckworth at the divisional headquarters in the ramparts just inside the Lille Gate, and after considering the best position to occupy when we went into the line, it was decided I should go to the advanced dressing station on the Menin Road just near the Burr Cross Roads.

On Sunday, November 18th, I said the First Mass for our brigade in one of the huts of the 5th Battalion near Café Belge, and went back to Dickebusch where the 148th Brigade troops heard Mass in the same hut I had used the week before.

On Tuesday, November 20th, I went up to the A.D.S. on the Menin Road, where we had a small " elephant " hut in which Padre Watt, the C. of E. padre, and myself were to sleep. There was room for a stretcher for each one, and some blankets, so we were well off for our sleeping accommodation.

The mess and dressing station were in well-sandbagged " elephant " huts on the other side of the road beside some half-ruined buildings. The country here was exactly the same shell-shot desolate area as on the other side of Passchendaele, and stretched away over Westhoek Ridge on to Broodsinde and Zonnebeke. The next morning our servants woke us at 4 o'clock to go up with the relief, so that we could get around before the enemy began his heavy shelling, which generally began about 10 o'clock. We were just eating a thick slice of fat bacon crushed between two slices of bread, with a can of warm tea before going, when Padre Watt, looking round on the party, said cheerily : " The condemned men ate a hearty meal." " Well," I said, " if that isn't the limit ! "

We started out in thick darkness in a tempest of rain ; the only chance of seeing anything was the

Verey lights the enemy put up now and then, for which we were grateful, as at least it showed us where we were.

All went well till we turned off on to the plank track at Burr Cross Roads; limbers and all sorts of traffic were struggling along in the darkness, the sickly smell of decaying horseflesh told us the road was decked with horrors the darkness hid from us. A crash and splash of flame in the blackness on the left and fragments rattling off our steel helmets caused the driver of the limber in front, evidently a new hand, to pull up short, the men behind cursing and calling on him to go on; he still hesitated, when another shock and crash, with its splash of flame, closer than the last, caused him to whip up his horses and go forward. We all pressed after him to get past the danger-point as quickly as possible. The rattle of machine guns sounded away on our right, and when we reached Westhoek Ridge, a grey light was just beginning to spread over the sky and herald the coming dawn. At 6 o'clock we reached our battalion headquarters, a concrete shelter past a great bump of brown rising out of the endless array of shell craters. We went forward along the duck-boards to A Company to bury one of the men killed during the night, and then, leaving Padre Watt, I went forward to our 6th Battalion, giving Holy Communion to some of our boys on the way. One came up out of one of the shell-holes in which our boys were sheltering, with the question, "Where will the Catholic service be held, Father?" I looked round at this wild expanse of unending desolation, with no shelter save shell craters to be seen: "Well," I said, "all we can do is to give you Holy

Communion where you are." So I dropped down into his shell-hole. A little later I left him quite happy and contented.

The trench mortars were in part of the shelter occupied by the 6th Battalion, and here the Catholics were able to come together with comparative safety, as the shelter was constructed of reinforced concrete covered with a thick layer of earth, and at a comparatively short distance it became easily blurred in the general tones of colour by which it was surrounded.

Coming back I met some field artillery. Several of their guns had been knocked out and blown to pieces. I went round to the shelters and gave Holy Communion to the Catholics, and then, as the shelling became rather heavy, began to make my way towards Westhoek Ridge. The shelling which began on the duckboards just past Zonnebeke continued until I was just over the Westhoek Ridge. Some engineers were waiting for me at the A.D.S., as they had heard there was a Catholic priest there. Father Guinness had been up working untiringly and going everywhere to let men know where the priest could be found.

The next day I went over the area round Halfway House and Hell Fire Corner: I had just reached the latter point when an officer came up and asked if I was a priest. He was working with a labour company on the railway near by, and after making his confession and receiving Holy Communion, he took me to the railway, where I was kept busy some time hearing confessions. Afterwards the men lined up behind the shelter of one of the trucks, and under the grey sky made their Communion.

Their expressions of gratitude were touching in the extreme. Many of them had been long without the Sacraments owing to the circumstances of their work. The officer invited me to visit the company headquarters near Ypres, and I promised to do so the next day.

Early the following morning I set out once more over Westhoek Ridge and past Anzac Point towards Zonnebeke. We were caught under heavy fire at the old point on the road up, and then set off along the duckboards and finally reached the 7th headquarters by following the white tape; they had an exceedingly contracted pill-box which that morning had just had a direct hit on the top from a 5·9. The earth was disturbed and the concrete roof cracked but not broken through, and happily no casualties. We went on to the 6th headquarters, where some men were awaiting burial. The digging of the grave was interrupted first by enemy planes and then by shells. While this was going on I spent some time in the other part of the dugout with our trench mortars. "What!" said one of the officers, "you going on leave in a few days, and coming up here! I wouldn't come within a hundred miles of this if I was going on leave." I may mention that there was quite a feeling amongst men in the line that if you were going on leave you would, if you went up, get knocked out, so once leave was through, men tried to keep as far back as possible; and certainly there was something to be said for their contention, for many were knocked out with the leave-warrant in their pockets, and there was the memory of the leave-train caught by enemy fire at Poperinghe, when nearly forty men were killed and wounded just as the train was moving out of the station.

After having gone round the shell-holes to give Communion to the 6th, the burial being completed, we began to think of getting back. I looked in to say good-bye to the trench mortars. " Look out as you go back; you are going to have a warm time," said they as we set out. And they were quite right. Shells fell promiscuously in all directions as we made our way back to the foot of Westhoek Ridge, where we were to strike the plank road. As we approached it I noticed there was not a living soul to be seen along it. All traffic had disappeared, an ominous sign in these parts. " You see that road," said I to Padre Watt. " Yes," said he, " there's nobody on it." " No, and we ought not to be on it either." I had scarcely spoken the words when a 9·2 shell crashed over, and then they came on two and three at a time in quick succession. I looked forward to the top of the ridge, that seemed an interminable way off, hoping that once we got the other side we should be clear. But even as I looked, little clouds of white smoke arose from behind it, which I vainly hoped came from our light railway. But, alas, when we reached the top and looked down the way to Burr Cross Roads the whole route was swept by bursting shells. " There's nothing to do but go on. *In manu Dei sumus.* If He wants us to come through or wants us to go it's all the same." We pressed on. A shell struck the road full in front; the plank beams flew up in the air like ninepins. " Look there ! " exclaimed Padre Watt. And I looked back to see the ammunition dump go up in a mass of cloud and flame just behind us. Over our shoulder came the shrieking shells. "We must look out and get clear of that point where they had the road," I said. Just as we reached it the shrill sharp shriek told us the shell was on us. Happily it struck the earth to the right. Showers of earth and rubbish poured down upon us, but neither of us was hurt. I looked forward and saw that by turning to the left we could escape the shells which were sweeping the road all the way. They were bursting in Bellevue Lake, sending up green showers of water. At last the road was reached and we turned sharp to the left, and in a few minutes had left the shells behind us. We met two artillerymen who had been quietly watching us come down the ridge, betting as to which shell was going to have us.

We both got back a little exhausted after a strenuous morning, fully realising how mercifully God had cared for us.

Everybody will remember that plank road piled up on either side with smashed guns, overturned limbers, dead mules and horses, and all the indescribable wreckage that characterised every one of the tracks that led up to our forward posts. There were no trenches, only shell-holes which, by linking two or three together, gave a shelter to the platoons with their officers; so the sufferings of the men, when these were half-filled with water, may be imagined, as no one dare leave them by day for fear of giving the position away to the enemy.

One incident will give an idea of the keenness of enemy observation: a young officer in one of these shelters got out in daylight and walked back to headquarters to make some report. He was relieved that night, but the enemy dropped a big shell into the shelter the next morning and killed the whole party.

In the afternoon I walked back to the labour company I had promised to visit at the other side of Ypres; all the men were waiting for me and a tent was provided. One by one the men stepped in and made their confessions. One of the last said to me: " Father, I have a friend wants to come, but he's been away so long he's afraid to come in alone: may I come in with him?" "Of course, dear boy." He disappeared and in a minute returned with the lost sheep. "Here he is, Father; now I leave him to you." The joy of reconciliation soon filled the penitent's heart.

Then all the men streamed in for Holy Communion. Just two candles gave light enough to see, as the men knelt around the improvised altar. I spoke a few words to them, and after Holy Communion we sang a few hymns and I gave Benediction. The men pressed eagerly around as I came away, and the hearty " God bless you, Father," " Thank you for coming, Father," showed that war had here deepened the appreciation of eternal things.

The moonlit night was favourable for aircraft, and the enemy bombed heavily all the way back, and when we reached the A.D.S. we found he had planted some shells in the infantry billet on the side, blown up the cookhouse and killed and wounded a number of men.

On Sunday I said Mass for some labour companies in one of their tin huts. The men had kindled a fire as it was inexpressibly cold, with a keen cutting wind driving in everywhere. We were all packed together, and with the help of the fire managed to keep from freezing. Thence I went into Ypres and said Mass in the big building called the Magazine, formerly used as an ammunition store—hence the name. A big shell-hole just in front of the hastily constructed altar gave us light and more ventilation than we needed. On my return to Menin Road, a soldier was waiting to be instructed in the Catholic religion and make his first confession and Communion; there was no time to lose, so I took him into our " elephant " dugout and there managed to teach the essentials, and he made his first Communion very joyfully. I set him up with some books of instruction, prayer-book, etc., and so bade him God-speed. He was wounded afterwards and wrote to me later from England, thanking me again for the help I had given him on the Menin Road.

That night my leave came through, and next morning Father Guinness came up and relieved me and I went down to Café Belge to our transport lines. I said good-bye to the doctors in the mess there, who had all been extremely hospitable, jumped a lorry, and set off for Poperinghe.

CHAPTER VIII

FIRST LEAVE AND MENIN ROAD AGAIN

THE two things most eagerly looked forward to in France are leave and letters. Men looked forward for months to their leave, and cheered themselves by the thought of it, no matter what the conditions under which they were living; those few brief days represented to them the height of human ambition.

I set off towards Vlamertinghe; as I reached the corner by the church, a car pulled up and gave me a lift down into Poperinghe; I went to the officers' rest, where one obtained an excellent dinner, and waited till just on 2 o'clock the following morning for the leave-train. We made a splendid run and reached Calais about 6.30. I had a little time to spare and went off to the Anglo-Belgian Hospital, where I succeeded this time in finding our two Sisters Eileen and Hilda. We just had time for a few minutes' greeting, and then I made my way to the boat, which was packed with troops, all in wonderful spirits at the thought of soon seeing "Blighty." How our eyes strained for the first sight of dear old England! At last the white cliffs came in sight, and soon after we were into the harbour and alongside the pier. The train for London moved out of the station, and we were speeding on through the beautiful English scenery unscathed by war, looking supremely lovely in the afternoon light.

By half-past four we were at Victoria; less than an hour later I was in the hospital ward at the Patriotic School, with Father Charles Murphy. He was still worn and ill but making steady progress, and our meeting was a joyful one indeed. Thence I went to

St. Gregory's, and on to Cobham, where a wire had already told my mother I was on the way down. A rush down to Syon Abbey, in Devon, to spend a few hours with our Sisters there. How much had to be crushed into these fourteen days, that rushed by with the speed of lightning! My experience was that of all—leave passed like a dream, and I was in the train speeding back to the sea once more.

The scenes that met the eyes as the leave-train goes out are familiar to many now : the little groups talking of anything except what was in their minds ; the final wrench, the bright eyes that struggle to hold back the tears—all is gone like a flash, and the leave-train goes its silent way.

We had a very rough passage going back and were all tired when we got into Calais. I went straight to the Church of the Sacred Heart, where I met Father Bodard and Sisters Eileen and Hilda. I put up at a quiet little French hotel close to the church.

I said Mass early next morning. Father Bodard and Sisters Eileen and Hilda came to the entraining point just outside the town. The train moved off ; there was a last farewell, and we were once more on our way up the line. The train took us back at a splendid pace, and we reached Poperinghe by 3 o'clock in the afternoon ; indeed, we travelled so quickly that we all said the Germans must have broken through. " It seems quite home-like to hear the guns again," remarked an artillery officer who was going back with me. I crossed over to the officers' rest, to find it had been blown up by a couple of bombs, and the interior a mass of wrecked furniture.

I jumped a lorry, and halfway towards Vlamer-

THE MENIN ROAD AGAIN

tinghe caught sight of some of our 5th Battalion officers. I got off and found we had just gone back into the line at the old spot on the Menin Road.

I slept with the transport that night, and set off next morning up to the A.D.S. and settled to take over next day. The day following I spent arranging with our men for the coming Sunday, the last I was to spend on the Ypres front, although I had no idea of it at the time.

We were placed in an exceptionally desolate expanse, and my old friends the trench mortars were trying to get a fire of sorts to warm themselves in their very cold surroundings. The 5th Battalion too fared rather badly.

I was back once more in the " elephant " hut by the dressing station; nothing had changed while I had been away—not even the weather.

Sunday morning I said the first Mass in a hut off the Menin Road, as a shell had blown up the old tin hut of the labour company I had used before. The hut was one of a series just finished as an extension of the dressing station. It was very crowded, and being semicircular, had its disadvantages; but it was rain-proof and fairly shell-proof, and was well sandbagged on top of the concrete. The second Mass I said over in Dragoon Camp, around which most of our brigade were lying. It was my last Sunday with them. In the evening I went over to give Benediction to my friends of the labour company on the Ypres Road.

A day later we were relieved and went back well beyond Café Belge, halfway to Halifax Camp.

The weather changed and a sharp frost transformed the roads completely, and our feet rang out sharply on the hard-frozen ground. I was out all day visiting our brigade and other units lying near us.

On Wednesday orders came to proceed at once to the 47th Division, so I had to rush round and say a hasty farewell to the warm-hearted North Country boys, with whom the days had passed so happily.

I went into Ypres, that City of the Dead, and its vast ruins appeared sadly beautiful in the light of the winter's morning. The great scarred rock-like ruins of the Cloth Hall still raised themselves defiantly against all the artillery of the enemy. I said farewell to Major Duckworth and others at the divisional headquarters, and turned round to leave Ypres behind me with a strange sense of regret.

I went over to Reninghelst and met Padre Patterson, who had always, as divisional chaplain, shown me every kindness, and had been ever ready to see that every Catholic had the right and opportunity of practising his religion, often riding out long distances to ascertain the hours of Mass in the village churches for those troops who were not able to be reached by the regular chaplains.

The journey down to Albert was cold and cheerless. I spent one night at Etaples, and continued the journey early next morning, reaching Albert in the afternoon.

CHAPTER IX

ON THE SOMME FRONT

A WHITE mantle of snow covered the ground when the train drew into the station of Albert. We dropped our baggage on to the platform and got it across the track to the baggage office; then went to the small hotel just outside, where we obtained a good lunch at a reasonable price.

Albert at that time had not suffered very much; the houses at the cross-roads had been demolished and the great church was considerably battered; the famous iron Virgin still bent forward on the summit of the tower, a familiar object, around which legend has woven the story that when the iron Virgin fell the war would end.

We set out along the road towards divisional headquarters, and the winter's day closed in long before we reached our destination. The Town Major of one of the villages *en route* provided us with tea and toast—very acceptable on that intensely cold winter's afternoon.

At headquarters it was arranged that for the time I should go to the 4th London Field Ambulance; a car took me to Senlis, where the ambulance was resting. I arrived in time for dinner, and received a kindly welcome from the officers there.

Father Bickford, the divisional chaplain, arranged for me to go to the 7th Battalion, so Monday morning I set out for the brigade headquarters at Ribemont, where some of the battalions were quartered. It was Christmas Eve when I arrived, so I had little time to arrange for the Christmas festival; nevertheless, we sang midnight Mass in the old church, and the bells were rung that night for the first time during the war. The brigade interpreter and four of the men of the trench mortar battery kept the peal going for nearly half an hour before midnight. The second Mass followed at 10.30 on Christmas Day.

The troops had only recently come out of the battle of Cambrai and the desperate struggle in Bourlon Wood; casualties had been extremely heavy, and there was the shadow of quiet restraint on the Christmas festivities. The battalion dinner for the officers of the 7th Battalion was held in one of the large farm-houses that made up the village. The evening was a very enjoyable one. The health of the officer commanding (Colonel Greene) was proposed, and he rose to make a reply : " I don't know quite what to say on an occasion like this," he said. " Something humorous would be out of place, and I don't want to make you sad "—his mind was back with the boys who had fallen so bravely such a short while before; he hesitated and his voice trembled a little—" You're a fine body of officers and I'm d—— proud of you ! " he said and sat down abruptly.

We remained in the area until January 10th; the weather all the time was intensely cold, and the only way to keep even moderately warm was to keep in constant motion.

The 6th and 7th Battalions were in Ribemont and the 15th and 8th in Méricourt l'Abbé, while the machine gunners, trench mortars, and field ambulance lay at Heilly. This gave one plenty of walking and helped to keep one in good condition. During the latter part of the time I stayed with the 6th Battalion, in the company commanded by Captain Ordish. On January 9th there was a fairly heavy snowstorm, followed by a thaw, so when we set out for the station early next morning the roads were as slippery as glass; men kept falling down, and as they were carrying full packs, once down could not get up again till helped up by their comrades.

At the station we waited patiently from 8 till nearly 12 o'clock, and at last our cattle trucks came in; we managed to make ourselves comfortable by means of a brazier and some wood which we annexed from a dump on the railside during a halt; at another place we got coal; so by the time our journey came to an end we were as warm and comfortable as circumstances would permit. The journey ended late in the afternoon and we marched to Lechelle, where we were quartered in good huts, and although the accommodation was not luxurious, we passed a good night there. A day's rest and then we marched off on our way to the trenches as the evening was closing in.

At Ytres we entrained on the narrow-gauge railway, and sitting around on the knife-edge of the little open trucks, after a while fell into a sort of stupor produced by the intense cold. It was 6 o'clock, and night had come on ere the train drew up at Trescault, and we ploughed our way through a field of mud and half-melted snow to the roadway.

Here our cookers were drawn up and hot tea served out; this was supremely welcome, and helped to restore some heat to our half-frozen bodies.

The night was intensely dark. I had not been able to see a yard in front of me since I got the gas at Nieuport, in fact I had to feel in front to lay hold of the hot mug of tea held out to me; so I looked forward a little anxiously to the march along the roads and up through the trenches to our dugouts.

That night was one of the most wonderful instances of the intervention of Sister Teresa of Lisieux that I have experienced, and they have been many during my time on the battle front.

Just before we fell in I said to her: "Sister, if I'm to come out of this alive, you will have to be my eyes to-night. You know I can't see, and so it's for you to help me."

We moved off in the darkness for our long tramp to Ribecourt, and from that moment a light shone from above my head that showed everything on the road quite clearly for about one hundred yards in front. I could see all our troops moving up and the others coming down, and the formation of the roadway. I looked up straight overhead to see whence it came, but no light was to be seen there; yet all the while I looked forward the light showed from above me and I was able to see quite clearly.

The journey up in the night, the tramp of the men, the occasional rumble of a ration limber returning, or a detachment of men going down, and the lookout for guides, the occasional illumination from a Verey light—these are familiar to all who have experience of the tramp up to the trenches.

We marched through Ribecourt, turned off by German House into the deep trench that zigzagged up to Kaiser Trench. These were the old German defences of the famous Hindenburg Line, and very deep. As we plunged into them a stream of water was pouring down; the light still followed me, and the white flow of water showed the way quite distinctly.

Sometimes it was too deep and we had to climb up the side of the trench to get along; the Verey lights went up, giving a brilliant light, yet instead of everything going black after the Verey light went out, as usually happens, I was able to see with perfect clearness right up to the entrance of our dugout in Kaiser Trench.

As I write, the memory of that night is as vividly before me as if I was treading the same way again, with the same light shining above me.

I owe very much in various circumstances of my life to the help and intercession of Sister Teresa of Lisieux, especially during the War, but on no occasion have I had a more evident manifestation of her power than this.

We clambered up the side of the trench and turned to the entrance of our deep dugout: the steps clogged with mud, but we reached the bottom of the shaft without mishap. The dugout had the disadvantage of having only one entrance, and was long and narrow with bunks arranged along the side.

This was the aid post, and the men we had come to relieve were all ready to go; the handing over was soon completed, and shortly after midnight we lay down and were soon asleep.

The next morning (Sunday) I gave Communion to some of our men in various parts of the trenches. Monday morning I went round the entire line. A sharp frost had hardened the trench bottoms, so I was able to get along easily enough and gave Holy Communion to nearly all our boys. When I reached the front trench I saw Colonel Neeley with his runners and one or two others walking right out in

No Man's Land quite unconcerned; only occasionally did a bullet come singing by.

The ground was still covered with snow and the enemy lines looked remarkably peaceful that bright winter's day.

There was little shelling of the front trenches that day, or indeed at all during the time we were in the line; nearly all the shells went over us back to Ribecourt and Trescault.

The weather unfortunately changed again and the thaw began in real earnest. The sides of the trenches caved in, the mud in them rose above our knees—thick slimy mud of quite a special type, a different sort from that of the Ypres salient. It dragged off the men's boots, socks, and waders; quite a number came down barefoot, having had puttees, boots, and socks sucked off by the mud.

The sickness began to increase, and the space in the aid post became so cramped that it was arranged I should go down to Ribecourt. The afternoon light was failing as we set out, and the trenches in such a state that we determined to go over the top the whole way down. There was little shelling, and we reached Ribecourt about 4 o'clock. We looked in at the advanced dressing station in German House, and then went on to brigade, finally found a cellar where we spent the night. The next day we shifted into the cellars opposite German House. Ribecourt was shelled pretty continuously every day with high explosive and gas shells, and although the troops in the front trenches were brought back each two days for a "rest," it was anything but a rest, and they were glad to get back to the comparative security of the front-line trenches.

The weather was bad all the time. I managed to give Benediction in one of the cellars in German House, and to those of our troops who were back in the village.

I went over to Father Bickford at the dressing station at Havrincourt, which, like Ribecourt, had a pretty good share of shells, and spent the day there.

After six days in Ribecourt I went up to the trenches again with Captain Ordish. The day before we went up the village was very heavily shelled; but when our time came to move up, the firing died down, although it had continued up to the moment when we were forming up to move forward, and once or twice the assembled troops had to seek shelter from the flying splinters.

We got up into our position without incident, and found our dugout was an exceedingly good one, with two entrances and plenty of room. We only remained two days, and were relieved on the evening of January 24th, 1918.

That morning I went round the line with Captain Ordish; the front was extraordinarily quiet; the country bathed in brilliant sunshine; high overhead the lark was singing, and it was difficult to believe that the enemy was only a few hundred yards away. We had a good view of Marcoing, which did not appear greatly damaged. As we turned back, a few shells began to fall over on Welsh Ridge, disturbing a number of crows settled in a field; they rose in the air as the shell burst, and almost immediately after were on the ground again as if nothing had happened. We began to move out along the road to Ribecourt about half-past seven that night, and then to Trescault, where after a long wait we got on the narrow-gauge railway and travelled down to Bertincourt, one of the ruined villages of the Somme area, which we reached at 2.30 a.m., weary and numbed with cold, after striving to balance ourselves for hours on the knife-edge of the little open trucks. However, everyone was in good spirits, and the band played us in to the tune of "Far from the Old Folks at Home," which fitted the situation rather well, and was just what we were all thinking.

The weather these days was raw and cold, and both Bertincourt and Ruyalcourt, where our brigade was quartered, could boast of a superabundance of mud if nothing else. Both villages had been wrecked and were mere ruins, but out of such we managed to form a fair number of shelters. We were bombed regularly every night, and generally fell asleep to the cheery sound of falling bombs and shrieking of anti-aircraft guns.

The Divisional Follies, a small troupe of players, were giving their entertainment one night in the large shed erected for recreation, at which practically the whole of the divisional officers were present. One of the singers was just concluding his song, when a terrific crash at the side of the hut shook the whole building and showers of brickwork came rattling on the roof; the singer's eyes went up to the roof anxiously, but he bravely finished his song, and as he retired the " principal girl " sprang on and picked up the next song instantly; for a moment I forgot she was a boy, and said to myself, " How plucky of her! " The poor singer went down badly wounded on the Somme later. I was standing at the A.D.S. in the Albert Road when a familiar face looked up from a stretcher at me: " Don't you remember me ? I was the principal girl in the divisional show when you used to come in and talk to us up at Bertincourt."

Nothing else untoward occurred to mar the performance, but it was quite enough for one night; the other bombs dropped far away, and although as usual the planes came over us more than once again that night, the bombs did not fall near enough to disturb our sleep.

On Sunday evening we got the news that, owing to the reorganisation of the army, three of our battalions were to be disbanded, news that we could hardly believe to be true at first, but which soon received ample confirmation. Officers and men were alike angry and indignant, but nothing could be done. They had been together all through the war; traditions had grown up around the battalions, and now they were all to be scattered amongst strangers. This change of organisation had something to do with the disaster that overtook our arms barely two months later, as there had not been sufficient time to allow of the absorption of the disbanded troops in their new units ere the storm of March 21st broke upon us with all its fury.

The only unit that remained undisturbed through this convulsion was the field ambulance; so on Monday I set off to spend some time with them till the work of rearranging the brigade was completed.

I walked to the C.C.S. at Ytres junction, where I expected to get a car on to the ambulance, but found they were a considerable way back, and as it was impossible to proceed that day, the C.O. at the

21st C.C.S. put me up for the night, and I got a good bed for the first time for many months. The next day I took train from Ytres junction and arrived in the afternoon at Maricourt, or rather at a siding in the desolate Somme country without any signs of a town in sight, or any signs of life save a few timber sheds beside the line. I was in doubt as to whether this was our destination or not, but one of the men by the huts informed me this was Maricourt, so we tumbled our belongings out on to the track and, leaving them there, set out to find the field ambulance.

After some time we came across some ruined buildings and huts where the ambulance was established. We had a kindly welcome from Colonel Williamson and the rest of the staff, and Corporal Guly came back with a hand-truck to pick up our baggage and bring it along.

I spent nearly three weeks with the ambulance at Maricourt, once a large and prosperous village; little now remained except one or two isolated houses, as it had been entirely razed on the enemy retirement the previous year; so completely that the rank vegetation which had covered the ruins entirely concealed them from view, and to a casual observer it seemed impossible to believe that a fairly large village had occupied that site less than two years ago. The divisional rest camp was established a short distance from the ambulance, and as large numbers of sick were constantly coming down, between the rest camp and the various labour companies scattered over the area, I found my time fully occupied.

The battle tide had rolled away. The long line

of white trenches, all silent and forsaken, and the ever-recurring white crosses, were all that remained as reminders of the bitter struggle that had raged over the land in 1916.

The winter sun shone brightly from the frosty sky during those February days, when in company with Captain Ironside I wandered across that battle-scarred area, over which brooded a silence, intensely sad and unearthly; indeed, I have never been so impressed with the sorrowful side of the war as in this silent rolling country of the Somme, its desolation accentuated by the destruction of the many woods that had once relieved the barrenness of the chalk hills.

A French infantry regiment had erected a very pretty little wooden chapel in a cemetery near the rest station; and there I said Mass weekdays and Sundays.

With what wonderful rapidity does nature strive to cover up the ruin man has wrought! Here the whole shell-pocked area was already overspread with tall grass, intermixed with strange patches of dark red vegetation, which, as the colonel remarked, reminded one of the blood of the slain.

On February 14th there was a gathering of Catholic chaplains to meet Father Rawlinson at Bapaume. I picked up a car to Albert, and then another on to Bapaume; on every side, as we passed, the white crosses stood out, memorials of the great price that had been paid to win this desolate region. Bapaume had been very badly damaged, most of the houses blown up and burnt during the enemy retreat, and was simply a reproduction of Ypres on a smaller scale. A considerable number of chaplains came together, and we spent a most interesting afternoon.

About half-past four I made my way to the crossroads to look for a lift homewards: the policeman on duty cheerfully told me there was no hope of a lorry that time of day. I just said a prayer to little Sister Teresa, and the very first lorry that followed took me into Albert; here things looked more hopeless still, but a word to Sister Teresa again, and a lorry appeared, which carried me to the door of our mess in Maricourt.

Just towards the end of my stay, we went over to Péronne, another town that had been in great part destroyed during the spring retreat. The beautiful flamboyant church had been blown up, in common with the rest of the town. The day of our visit was one of those beautiful spring days that, even to such a picture of desolation as this, give a sense of sad beauty which the beholders can never forget.

The work in this area, amongst little groups of men belonging to engineers, labour companies, and the like, was particularly consoling, as my visits gave them the only opportunity of receiving the Sacraments for many months; being entirely isolated and away from any large bodies of troops, no chaplain had been in their neighbourhood for a long time.

My stay with the ambulance came to an end on February 20th, and I left with much regret. Their car took me into Bertincourt, where I joined the 17th London Regiment, one of the new battalions in the reorganised brigade. The next day we marched through Bus, Lechelle, and Etricourt, to

Equancourt, where we settled down for a few days; then went to the camp near Barastre, and finally returned to Equancourt, where we remained until we moved into the line just before the great German attack on March 21st. Our battalions were spread out between Equancourt, Etricourt, and Manancourt, the 15th Battalion being at Manancourt and the 17th in Equancourt, and the 21st in hutments just beside them.

Scattered about were a number of engineers and other units, for whose spiritual wants one was able to provide, the officers always welcoming one's efforts and doing all in their power to help. Few Benedictions have been more consoling than those given in those bare little huts with just a table covered with an army blanket and the very minimum of ritual accessories possible. The men grouped closely together and singing with wonderful earnestness, and then the general Communion following. As these companies were working both weekdays and Sundays, I found the only way to do anything for them was to fix a service in their own camp in the afternoon, after their return from work, for it was out of the question to expect men tired out with heavy labour to walk any distance at the end of the day.

On March 8th we moved back again to Equancourt, and I had for my quarters a fairly large recently-built brick hut; Sergeant Doherty and some others set to work and erected quite a presentable altar of sandbags, with a trench-grid covered with canvas to form a *Mensa*, and here every night a devout little congregation assembled for Rosary and Benediction.

The weather most of the time was intensely cold but fine, so that one was able to reach our rather widely spread out brigade without difficulty.

Meanwhile rumours were pretty constant of the coming German attack; trenches and wiring were appearing in all directions, big guns kept coming up, and there was a general sense of tense expectancy pervading the army.

I remember looking at the trenches being hastily dug at Manancourt, and thinking the labour rather wasteful, so little did the likelihood of the enemy breaking through and coming so far back appeal to one. Meanwhile our troops had been constantly practised in the defence of the lines before Fins in the direction of Metz-en-Couture.

Passion Sunday came—the last Sunday before the great storm was to break upon us. I said Mass first for our two battalions at Equancourt, and then went across-country to the large wooden hut beside Vallulart Wood, for the 15th and part of the other brigade. In both places, in view of the fact that we were expecting to go into the line very soon, the troops all made their general Communion. I spoke a few words exhorting them all to courage and entire confidence in God : " What is before us we cannot tell, but we know nothing can befall us that the providence of God does not permit "; and so we prepared for the days of conflict coming towards us so swiftly.

On Monday evening, March 18th, we assembled for our last Benediction in the little hut, a place now associated with many holy memories, and we all felt a keen sense of regret at leaving it.

Next morning I said the last Mass I was destined

to say for some time. Just as we were getting ready for our move to Metz, I got a call to Rocquigny to meet the army chaplain, so I had to make my way there, walking the greater part of the way, getting a lift on a lorry for the remainder.

CHAPTER X

THE MARCH OFFENSIVE

I LEFT Rocquigny late in the afternoon and got as far as Lechelle, where the 4th Field Ambulance provided me a lodging for the night. The front was quiet, ominously so, and gave little idea of what was coming. Indeed the latest information we had led us to believe the enemy was postponing his offensive till May.

Early next morning, March 20th, I set out for our camp near Metz; one of the ambulance cars gave me a lift into Metz, another of those destroyed Somme villages that had once been fair and prosperous, now levelled to the ground, save for a few ruined houses still standing. I found our battalion in tents and huts in a field on the right of the road between Metz and Fins.

There was a small Catholic chapel in the village, where I put up notices for Mass on Sunday following, as I decided to walk back from the line and say Mass for the brigade resting in support at Metz, and told our quartermaster to leave my Communion set with the Town Major; happily he did not carry out my instructions, or it would have been lost in the retreat. The day was bright and cold, with a few clouds sharply defined drifting across the sky. Colonel Parrish had arrived and taken over command of the battalion a few days before. Major Beresford was second in command, and Lieutenant Thorogood adjutant.

Towards evening we began to prepare for our forward move; while we were doing so, a few shells fell around the camp, some rather near.

The clear cold spring day was drawing to a close as we fell in and moved up towards the line; a few shells were bursting over the low hills in front as we went forward, but we got into our positions without any untoward incident.

The German dugouts which were to serve our battalion headquarters proved excellent in every respect, and we congratulated ourselves as being so well housed for our twelve days in the trenches. We got finally settled in about midnight, and I went to stop the night with Dr. Douglas, a young American M.O. who had recently joined the battalion, in the cellar in Villas Pluich which served for the regimental aid post.

This was situated a few hundred yards in front of the trench in which headquarters were established, so that we could easily go there for meals, while we slept at the aid post. The first night we were fearfully crowded, as the doctor, myself, and half a dozen orderlies all slept huddled up together in the small cellar, as best we could.

That was the night of March 20th–21st, and I shall never forget the dawning of that St. Benedict's Day.

About 5 a.m. the roll of the artillery, which had been moderate during the night, became very intense; the crash and rush of shells became blended in one grand ceaseless tempest of sound, which continued without diminution till late in the afternoon.

About 7 o'clock that morning my orderly, Eyre, went out to get some water, and returned very sick, saying that the air was full of gas. About half-past eight we all set out along the road to our trench for breakfast. A thick mist covered the country, we could only see a short way along the road; the heavy air was filled with the fumes from the smoke screens put over by the enemy, and I experienced a strange dizzy sensation in the head and nearly fell as we went along the way.

Overhead the rush of thousands of shells of every calibre, with the crash of their bursting on either side, produced an intense volume of noise such as I had never heard before. It was no ordinary barrage, and we realised that the great attack had begun.

At headquarters we got very little news, for most of the lines were cut, and we were out of touch with our front line: it was said the enemy had taken some 200 yards of our front, and two companies of our battalion were sent forward to retake the lost ground; but before they had got very far, to our surprise the movement was countermanded from division. As the day wore on the sun broke through and the mist lifted, and we could see for quite a considerable distance; everywhere shells were bursting, and still the same ceaseless din overhead. Sergeant Doherty found a small shelter in which I could hear the men's confessions and give them Holy Communion; it was by no means the safest of places, as it was our bomb store and on the roadside; but it was quiet and convenient, and there a number of men came to receive the Sacraments.

Late in the afternoon, the Church of England chaplain of the 21st Battalion joined us; he was able to bring little news, and only added to the general impression that the long-expected offensive had begun at last.

I was standing looking out towards the forward positions, when a sergeant pointed out on the horizon some small figures coming over the ridge.

I stood watching them some time, wondering at our men walking about in that heavy fire. As we watched, the figures continued to move forward, and the next minute I saw the S.O.S. signal going up beside me. The front lines had gone, and the figures we had seen were those of the oncoming enemy. In a few minutes the men were manning the trenches, headquarters staff officers and men waiting rifle in hand, while a short distance along the Lewis guns began to speak. We sat up on the top of the trench, watching and waiting, as the day closed in ; the men remained in their firing positions, but darkness came, so we went down the dugout and had our dinner as usual, and began to think the situation was not so very serious, as, after all, only a small proportion of the line had gone as far as our front was concerned, and we knew absolutely nothing of what was happening elsewhere, although we were puzzled at the counter-attack being countermanded. The shelling was slackening a little now, and although there were occasional alarms during the evening, nothing startling developed, and about 10 o'clock I went back with Douglas to our cellar for the night. This time most of the orderlies were sleeping back in the trenches and we had space to lie down with some degree of comfort. I determined to take off my boots and give my feet a little ease. Douglas said : " I'm not going to risk it." We settled down, and I was just falling into a pleasant sleep, when I heard footsteps stumbling down the steps and a voice saying : " Line gone. Enemy coming on. Get back to trenches as quickly as possible." We were on our feet and struggling into our boots very quickly. We collected our belongings with all possible speed, and a few minutes later we were swinging along the road through the mist and fog towards Plough Support, as our trench was called. Before morning the enemy were in the village, and our cellar had become one of his machine-gun posts.

When we reached headquarters everyone was already preparing to move, and soon after we set out towards Beauchamp, where the next stand was to be made. As we crossed the road the troops were already erecting barricades and hastily digging a trench across it.

We struggled along in the darkness through the trenches as best we could, finally climbed out and struck the open tract towards our new position. We were all stretched out in straggling order and found it difficult to keep touch in the fog. However, between 2 and 3 o'clock we reached the dugouts recently occupied by brigade, and by 4 o'clock, thoroughly tired out, we all lay down on the ground and slept on until 8 o'clock the following morning, a sleep occasionally disturbed by the intense cold.

Friday, March 22nd, was an exceptionally fine day. The early mist disappeared as the sun rose, and we obtained a good view of the surrounding country. The horse artillery were retiring from the direction of Trescault and Ribecourt, and we watched them moving along the roads; a shell would burst near by, and as the smoke cleared away we saw the batteries racing by as fast as the horses could gallop. The enemy fire continued very heavy throughout the day, and we received orders to fall back upon Metz that night. As the day wore on, all around the smoke rising from dumps being blown up gave evidence that the situation was becoming increasingly grave. Around and behind us these pillars of smoke rose high in the heavens.

Towards evening twenty-five enemy planes in battle array passed over us, a striking and impressive spectacle.

The engineers were to blow up our dugouts as soon as the evacuation was complete, and Major Beresford was to remain behind to see the work carried out, so I offered to stay behind to keep him company. By nightfall the charges had all been placed in position. We had dinner as usual, and by half-past eleven the headquarters company were forming up above-ground, ready to move, when a ring on the telephone brought us the first definite news of what was happening elsewhere.

The enemy had broken through at Gouzeaucourt and was approaching Fins, well behind us. " There isn't a moment to lose," said the colonel. We got above-ground with all speed and set out in the mist and darkness, which, however, was somewhat relieved by the shining of the Paschal moon, towards the Metz–Fins line.

As we went, Verey lights rose all around us, and we wondered if there was any way out at all; anyhow, if there was, the neck through which we must retire was undoubtedly very narrow, and growing narrower as the moments passed.

Heavy shells came over behind us, drawing closer as we moved along. We reached a sunken road and the company halted and sheltered in a hollow by the roadside. Here the colonel addressed a few words to the battalion: " Men of the 17th London: the enemy has broken through, and you have to hold him; there are some trenches not very deep, and you must dig for all you're worth and make them better, and you will succeed." We waited for the other companies to come up to us, and then just as our troops began to cross the road the enemy opened up his light artillery, and shells came over in rapid succession, falling on the men as they moved along. There were calls for stretcher-bearers, and as we passed one poor boy lying wounded by the side of the tract was calling out: "Take me to a place of safety." It seemed humorous when one thought how far from any place of safety we were.

The C. of E. padre knew the position and led us towards it; we stumbled on across the open fields, occasionally tangled in wire, and at last the trenches were reached. Machine-gun fire was fairly strong in the direction of Fins, and the occasional " ping " of the bullet sounded in our ears as it sped past.

The moon was setting when we finally took up the headquarters position in the Metz–Fins Road. The dugouts of the artillerymen, hastily abandoned, gave us shelter. The ambulance at Metz had been withdrawn, and I proposed to go to try and find the 4th Ambulance at Lechelle in the morning. Meanwhile we were all tired and exhausted, and Thorogood and myself found a shelter in which to get a few hours' sleep; it was very broken, as the cold was constantly waking us, but anyhow we had a little rest. The men meanwhile spent the night doing what they could to deepen and strengthen the trenches. The sky was lit up by the flames rising from the burning dumps, and rifle-firing continued intermittently all the night.

About half-past seven in the morning of the 23rd

we got up, stiff and cold, from our comfortless sleep, and went along to the dugout where the colonel and the rest of headquarters were resting. Here the servants prepared some hot tea, bread and biscuits, which helped to warm us a little. The sun was coming up and the day happily once more promised to be fine.

At first I thought of sending my servant over to try and find the ambulance, but he was not sure of the way, so we set out together. The bullets were singing over us as we went up the rising ground the other side of the sunken road; when we reached the top of the incline we found the 142nd Brigade digging in vigorously, and I felt things were more hopeful, although this favourable impression was soon to be dispelled.

We walked on and came down to Ytres junction by the side of Vallulart Wood. Here I first saw how serious the situation was. The great junction, generally the scene of so much activity, was absolutely deserted. Not a truck or locomotive to be seen. The silence and sense of abandonment were strangely uncanny. I found an artilleryman just getting a fire lighted in one of the deserted huts. " You won't find anyone here; they all hopped it last night," was the information he volunteered as we came up.

We crossed the rails and turned towards the C.C.S., but here again silence and abandonment; everything showed signs of hasty flight: clothing, stores, equipment, all left behind. The whole of the patients and staff had been hurriedly cleared during the night and early hours of the morning.

We moved on up towards the aerodrome. Here

once again silence. Not a plane to be seen. The great sheds standing empty and forsaken.

I looked down towards the huts occupied by the field ambulance, but no sign of life came from there. I left my servant here, as he was footsore and exhausted, and went forward. Heavy shells were dropping in steady succession into Lechelle as I approached. I entered the huts, but the weird uncanny silence showed that they too had been evacuated, and as it was impossible to form any idea of where they had gone to, I decided to return and get back to our battalion.

I turned back towards the C.C.S. When we arrived there we found a dressing station had been opened in some dugouts below the nurses' quarters, on the right of the road. I stopped and had a talk with one of the doctors, and asked him to send a couple of his men back with me to see the way to our position for getting down the wounded. Meanwhile I turned into the large store where a few ambulance men were resting, and we got a good supply of hot milk, bread and bully beef, for which we were very thankful, as the day was well advanced and we were beginning to feel exhausted.

Here, too, I bathed my feet and obtained new socks. While I was engaged in this operation, General Mildren came in : " What pity to leave all this ! But it can't be helped," he remarked. I apologised for the work on which I was engaged : " Excellent thing to do—excellent thing ! " With which remark he went out.

When we came out the dressing station had closed down and the staff disappeared ; wounded men were streaming down across the railway from the tract that led past Vallulart Wood. The ping-ping of passing bullets had become more constant, the enemy having worked right round through Equancourt.

We went forward to ascend the ridge, along the crest of which lines of figures were showing. Eyre, my orderly, was quite sure they were enemy troops, but it seemed to me impossible that the enemy could have advanced so far in so short a time; so we went forward, till an officer of the 21st met me and pointed out the position. He showed me our men halfway down the hill, while the enemy were coming over the top in considerable force. "Will you tell brigade we are running out of ammunition and cannot hold the valley unless we get more?" "Well, where is brigade?" "They are over there," he said—just behind the nurses' huts, pointing to the low buildings opposite the C.C.S.

I turned back, and after a while found General Kennedy with General Mildren and some of the staff sitting behind the hut watching the struggle across the valley through their glasses. As I appeared around the corner of the hut General Mildren exclaimed: "Get down, get down!" I had quite forgotten the bullets and dropped down. "Well," said General Kennedy, "what do you want?" "The 21st say they are running short of ammunition and cannot hold the valley unless they have a fresh supply very soon." "Who told you, anyone in authority?" "An officer of the 21st," I answered. "Very well." "What shall I do?" I asked. "You had better make your way in that direction," he said, pointing towards Rocquigny.

We turned away and began to ascend the incline towards the aerodrome. "Can you go any quicker?" said my orderly. "Not if a thousand machine-guns are behind me," I said. For the incessant walking was beginning to tell. As we went up, little groups of men were lying down and sighting their rifles, the barrels of which were pointing directly at us as we advanced. "I hope they don't fire till we get through them," I remarked as we pressed upwards, the ping-ping of the bullets following us all the way; we turned off a little to the left to avoid Lechelle and Bus, which were being heavily shelled. As soon as we had passed the aerodrome and began to descend the other side of the hill, we got free of the machine-guns. All sorts of men, guns, and transport were in motion across the fields towards Rocquigny.

I met a few men straggling along very exhausted. I stopped and helped them along, urging them forward if they wished to avoid falling into the enemy's hands. Some artillery had unlimbered and were sighting their guns in the open as we passed. As I continued my way, I gradually gathered together some sixty men of various regiments from our own brigades and some from other divisions. All had lost contact with their units and were utterly worn out and exhausted. I urged them to keep all together and halted frequently so as not to distress them. I had determined to make for Bapaume and get some instructions from the division in there, but an artillery officer I met strongly advised me not to attempt it as the enemy was already close to that town, and would probably be in it before we could reach it. So we pressed on into Rocquigny, hoping that we might find some divisional headquarters there. We arrived there only to find it already deserted, only two or three servants were left behind, hastily packing as much as they could hope to get away. They could give us no information, so there was nothing to do but to press on towards Sailly-Saillisel. I tried to cheer the men with the prospect of re-forming on the other side of the Bapaume–Péronne Road behind the Second Army, which rumour told us was taking up a position there, to cover our retreat, a rumour without the least foundation.

Marching and halting, at last we reached Sailly-Saillisel, on the Bapaume Road. I halted the men and left them while I went forward to find a divisional headquarters, which I was told was to be found somewhere near Le Transloy. What a scene met the eye when the road was reached: one solid slowly-moving mass of lorries, horses, limbers, guns, generals and staff officers in cars, ambulance wagons, all slowly pushing their way along. Would order ever come out of this apparently hopelessly confused mass? I saw for the first time what an army in retreat was like. I went up towards Le Transloy, and at the point where the Rocquigny Road joined it, found another stream pouring into the Bapaume Road. Here I met Padre Bohn and the quartermaster of the 4th Field Ambulance, who invited me to spend the night with them on the road to Lesbœufs. I found an officer of the 21st collecting the stragglers, and he took over the charge of the men I had collected.

The various transports were formed up in the fields by the roadside; indeed, the whole countryside was alive with every conceivable kind of troops and transport. Labour companies struggled along, trying to carry their heavy loads and save as much of their belongings as was possible. As night fell I set off along the road to Lesbœufs, which was filled like all the roads with one solid moving mass of every conceivable kind of traffic. We were footsore and exhausted, after being on our feet without rest for wellnigh twelve hours. The ambulance had moved back much farther than we expected and had well passed Lesbœufs. Luckily an ambulance car picked us up and took us to the field where the ambulance had just moved in as we arrived. After the hot day the night was proportionately cold. A few tents were pitched, and under shelter of one we had a meal of bully beef and bread. All through the night the moving mass never ceased to roll by, and the bursting shells drew ever nearer and nearer.

Early the next morning we rose and prepared to move forward again. Hot tea and bread and butter helped us on our way; and some artillery moved to take up their position behind us as we moved off the field and along the road once more. We had scarcely got clear before the enemy shells were bursting on the ground we had vacated.

About 11 o'clock we halted near some huts occupied by American troops; here we got a wash and shave—the first since the great offensive had begun. All sorts of rumours were afloat, but no authentic news was obtainable. After a short rest we moved off once more through the Somme country, now alive with hastily-erected camps, where from sheer exhaustion various units had been compelled to halt and rest awhile, a striking contrast to the tranquil silence that had reigned over it a few days before. Towards the afternoon the figure of the Virgin of Albert came in sight, and we received orders to halt and open a dressing station by the roadside. We turned into the field, tents were quickly pitched, and we were soon attending to the trickle of sick and wounded. We sat on the grass and had a hot meal, the first since the retreat began. Heavy explosions a short way back I took to be shells, others thought they were one of our heavy guns firing, so to settle the point I walked back up the hill a little in the direction of La Plato, where I could see stores were being blown up. I waited some time without anything happening, when a terrific crash behind me proved unmistakably the fact that it was a shell and not a gun. A great black cloud shot up from the road, and I hurried down, expecting in its conjested state to find there had been heavy casualties; happily only one man was wounded in the arm. That the serried moving mass escaped so lightly was little short of a miracle.

I went back to our encampment and reported that it was enemy shells and not our guns that were causing the explosions.

Night was just falling, and, thoroughly exhausted, we were going to rest, when the order came to strike tents at once and get to the other side of Albert that night.

The hum of enemy planes overhead sounded unpleasantly as we were forming up to move on to the road. Suddenly the ping-ping of machine-gun bullets caused us to drop into the trenches and get what cover we could until the plane had passed over.

We got on to the road at last, and by slow stages, with constant halts, moved towards Albert; streams of traffic were all converging on the cross-roads in the centre of the town and reduced movement more and more as night wore on. Indeed, it seemed we should never get through. Just as we approached Albert the enemy planes let fly their bombs, and great splashes of flame shot upwards as they burst amongst the houses.

Slowly onwards—a hundred yards and halt, moving and halting, we gradually approached the centre of the town. We halted just inside the town. " The planes are over us again," exclaimed someone, cheerfully, as at last, after what seemed like an age, we were past the cross-roads and moving out along the road towards Millencourt. We halted by a steep bank on the road, when a series of bombs burst close on the other side of the bank, lighting up the whole area. We crouched tight up against the bank, the fragments flew harmlessly over our heads, and we escaped without a single casualty. As soon as things were quiet, we pushed along up the road, halted a short distance from Millencourt, and turned into a field on the left. The enemy dropped one of his brilliant lights, which remained over Albert like a great arc lamp for nearly five minutes, lighting up the whole town and surrounding country. Relays of enemy planes passed over, bombing all through the night. We slept in the ambulance suffering acutely from the cold, alternately sleeping and waking every few minutes; it was an intense relief when dawn came at last, and some hot tea helped to warm our blood a little.

I went back along the road to Albert and found our transport on the right and men coming down. The whole brigade was moving back, and so I spent the morning seeing as many men along the road as I could, and collecting their postcards which they were eager to get sent off to assure folks at home of their safety.

That night I slept in Millencourt; our transport had taken up a position on the road to Bouzincourt, so I got my valise and hoped for a good night's rest. We turned in very early and slept soundly till about 4 o'clock, when we were awakened by orders to move at once. I woke my orderly and we went out to our transport drawn up on the road. The first light of day had not yet begun to show in the sky; great fires blazed along the horizon, rising from Rocquigny, Bapaume, and other towns; occasionally the steady burning was relieved by great flashes of fiery red as munition dumps blew up. The roll of guns was sounding away on the left, and in front the sharp crack of rifles and machine-guns. The scene was strangely, hauntingly impressive.

We moved forward a little and halted again, and the day at last began to dawn, fine but intensely cold. Some hot tea warmed us up a little, and then we moved off to Bouzincourt. We entered the village and found most of the inhabitants had already fled, leaving even their meals untasted on the tables, as well as all their belongings. The few people who remained stared at us with blanched, terrified faces, as our coming seemed to them to herald the approach of the dreaded foe. The French interpreters were busy urging the few remaining people to leave. Two poor old women said to me despairingly: " All we have is here; we can't leave. We have not a relative in the world. Can we stay ? " I inquired if they had a cellar, and as they answered in the affirmative, I told them, "Yes, but keep in the cellar if there is any firing." The rattle of machine-gun fire drew closer all the morning, so I went back to the high ground overlooking Albert, to see what I could make of the situation. The enemy was already in Albert, and pushing a little forward on our side. A few of our howitzers were in action, and on the top of the hill one could see little but the smoke rising from burning dumps and ruined villages.

A company of troops of all sorts, hastily hurried up from the rear, were just taking up their position; some of them were being instructed in the use of their weapons while I was there. So altogether the situation did not look too reassuring.

I went back to the village, where our men were forming up. Orders had come for us to fall back to Luvencourt. We left about 4 o'clock, and were scarcely clear of the village ere the enemy lay down his first artillery barrage upon it.

The long march was not over till nearly 8.30 that night. One of the most remarkable sights on the march was the blowing up of a big petrol dump on our right, terrible but magnificent.

Early next morning we received orders to prepare a position in front of Luvencourt: we were just getting to work when this was countermanded, and we had to proceed to Toutencourt, where the curé provided me with a good night's lodging. I said Mass in the church at 7 o'clock the next morning, for a few of our men who were near by; then we went forward to Warloy, which we reached in the afternoon. This was Holy Thursday, one of the strangest in our experience, for in the anxieties of these days we had almost lost count of the succession of time. But the news was now more reassuring, the enemy's advance was slackening, and the news from the rest of the front went to show that at last we were beginning to hold him.

It was only when we finally rested at Warloy that we were able to realise the extent of our losses. Lieutenant Thorogood had gone down severely wounded, and Major Beresford also. Captain Ordish, badly wounded, had been taken prisoner, and died soon after. Most of the remaining officers had been killed or wounded, while the casualties in the ranks had been very high.

CHAPTER XI

AT BOUZINCOURT

WE were resting at Warloy, after the exhausting fighting following on our retirement from the trenches before Cambrai, across the Somme and through Albert and Bouzincourt, when on Good Friday morning the order came that we must return and hold the line again in front of Bouzincourt. As we had been expecting to rest for a few days, I was looking forward to our men receiving Our Lord in comparative quiet on Easter Sunday, and now we had to go into action instead. I hurried to the curé's house, hoping that he would have the Blessed Sacrament in the church, but he, fearing the entrance of the enemy into the town, had consumed the Hosts, and my own ciborium had been exhausted during the retreat. For a moment I wavered in doubt as to what to do, but the curé said, "Of course I can't say Mass, but if you like to say Mass, to give your men Holy Communion, you have the church at your disposal." I decided at once that the need of the men must come before the ritual rule which forbade any Mass being said on that day, and determined to say Mass immediately and call the men together for Holy Communion at midday.

The men came together in the church, and, with the building vibrating to the crash of guns, we sang a few hymns that are great favourites of the men—"Sweet Sacrament Divine" and "Soul of my Saviour"—and then all knelt at the altar rails and received Our Blessed Lord. That Good Friday Communion will not be forgotten by those of us who survive. The church, a very simple but devotional building, exceedingly well cared for, in striking contrast to most of those in the Somme valley, appeared strangely beautiful to us after the desolated shelters in which we had worshipped so long. At the close I asked the men to recite one Hail Mary that God might spare this sanctuary in which we had that day received Our Lord. As a matter of fact, the church has never been touched, because that Easter marked the final arrest of the oncoming flood, and although the town has been shelled and heavily bombed since then, not even a window of the church has been broken.

We came out and prepared to go up to the line, and as evening was falling we moved forward, company by company. We passed through Senlis, and darkness had fallen before we reached the outskirts of Bouzincourt on our way to the ridge of Martinsart Wood. A few stray bullets whizzed by as we came along; one of the men caught a bullet in his leg, and walked on till we reached the wood, not realising he was wounded. He went to feel what was the matter with his leg, which had become rather stiff and painful, and found the bullet sticking out of it. The night closed in damp and cold and with rain falling. Our shelter was a hole dug in the chalk just by the roadside, a little galvanised iron covering and some pieces of canvas keeping the worst of the rain off; and here we slept huddled together during the night, the wind and rain beating on us, awakened every few minutes by the cold. Day dawned at last and the cooks prepared the customary hot tea, which was welcome indeed after the long cold night.

Meanwhile the enemy had begun to shell the ridge and valley and the village beyond, ranging promiscuously over the centre area. The doctor thought the position too near the road to be safe, and so we set out to find some other position. On the way I gave Holy Communion to the men of the headquarters staff. I found headquarters had a place partly excavated from the chalk, and completed by a bell tent fitted on to give a little more shelter from the elements. We chose a spot near the end of the valley in the direction of Englebalmer. The rain began to drizzle down and the shells began dropping around while we dug as hard as we could to form a shelter in the bank beside the road. Meanwhile, we had left the galvanised iron behind us and no guard, so when our men went to fetch it, of course some others had already " pinched it," " won it," or " scrounged it," as is the way in the army.

However, we soon " won " the property of somebody else, and by three in the afternoon had our shelter fitted up and crawled inside. Wet and muddy and cold, with the rain still coming down like a flood, it was a grateful shelter indeed.

The shells dropped cheerfully all round, the splinters fell harmlessly about, and so the day passed on. Just as darkness was falling a nose-cap from a shell near by landed on our roof, and we thought at first it was coming in on us, but the structure resisted well, and then we settled down for another night of alternate waking and sleeping, the wet and cold and our cramped position arresting our slumbers every few minutes the night long. My mind went back to the old days at St. Gregory's and the very different way Holy Saturday was spent then and now.

Easter morning broke chill and gloomy, but I was

out fairly early to carry Our Blessed Lord to the boys. Up the valley the men knelt in the mud and took off their helmets and received Holy Communion as if in church, in spite of the shells bursting close by and the splinters and fragments scattering over us. Then a call at headquarters: "A happy Easter to you!" made the colonel look up. He saw the humour of it and wished us a happier one next year. On then, and up the sides of the ridge to the boys who had striven to dig themselves some sort of shelter in the side, holding on to twigs and branches of bushes and trees to save oneself from slipping in the mud and falling headlong into the valley below. Everywhere the men came out, glad to receive their Lord on this strange Easter Day. One man was so overjoyed, he must open the letter he had written to his wife and tell her the good news that he had got his Easter Communion after all. Everywhere it was "a happy Easter," despite the miserable external surroundings; Catholics know that external surroundings count little; if they are in the Grace of God, that is all that matters.

The shells sang over us and fell into the valley or down into the village of Martinsart, and the enemy's observation balloon looked down on us and saw every movement in the valley: so our situation was not over-comfortable.

In the afternoon I went over to Englebalmer, the village behind Martinsart. I passed our artillery on the way and entered the village, and there I met one of our old Earlsfield boys, George Nadig, who had quite abandoned all hope of getting his Easter Communion. "Why, it's Father Benedict!" It was a happy meeting, all the happier because so unexpected. We spoke of old times, and within shelter of a shell-stricken house he made his Easter Communion. After a short while we parted, and I took my way back across the fields to our position in the dugout by the roadside. So passed the Easter of 1918. That night our relief came, and we made our way back down through the darkness to Senlis for a brief respite from the line.

As night was closing in the relief began to arrive, and the headquarters section moved up out of the wood on to the road down to Bouzincourt. The clouds hung overhead heavily and darkness fell quickly as we tramped along through the mud towards Bouzincourt; the firing had died down, and only an occasional shell sang over us as, chilled tired and exhausted, we pressed on, passing the ghostly figures of the relieving troops going up to take their turn in the line.

Bouzincourt had been badly knocked about since last we rested there, as we perceived even in the darkness; it was soon to suffer still more. We reached our headquarters, an underground cellar; and along one end of it we wedged in some beds of wood, wire, and canvas, roughly knocked together, yet very welcome indeed, as they kept us off the damp floor. Some small grated openings let in light and air to some extent, while the barrel roof of stone promised protection from shell fragments.

We waited till the rest of the headquarters staff arrived, which carried us on into the early hours of the next morning. Then we all lay down to rest, six of us wedged together. Colonel Parrish took his place with the rest and shared all our comforts and discomforts, and never through these trying days of hardship ever sought an easier lot for himself in things great or small than fell to us, while he generously made space in the very contracted headquarters for both the Church of England chaplain and myself. In spite, or perhaps because, of the discomfort, we all slept soundly till late the following day. The cook awoke us with a cup of ever-welcome tea, and how welcome it can be, despite its strength (for the servants were always very lavish in the amount of tea they used) and even tin mugs, those who have experienced life underground know full well.

The day broke grey and depressing, with rain falling steadily, and when we went above ground we saw everywhere evidence of the havoc and destruction the enemy shelling had caused; scarcely a house remained intact, and many were already a ruined heap of wood, bricks, and mortar. The shells fell around us the day long, with little respite, carrying still further the work of destruction.

The church had been badly damaged, the sanctuary shattered, and the whole interior was a scene of appalling desolation.

The colonel offered to send down such articles as we could save from the church that night, if we could get them back and put them on the ration limber. During a quiet interval my servant and myself made a dash for the church; we climbed up over the piled-up wreckage of the sanctuary and entered the sacristy behind it. With all speed we cleared the vestment presses, and gathered together everything of value and prepared to return to our headquarters. Just as we were ready to go the shelling recommenced, so we had to wait for a quiet interval to make our way back.

After some time the looked-for interval came, and we sped through the streets, over the ruins of fallen houses, back again to headquarters, where the vestments were quickly sewn up in canvas and directed to the care of the French Mission.

The next day proved fairly fine, and I got out and gave Holy Communion to Sergeant Doherty and others, and walked over to the village of Englebalmer to see the 4th Field Ambulance. I found Captain Gaston, the American doctor, and sat talking to him some while, little realising it was the last time I should see him alive.

The shelling was lively all the way back, two men being killed on the road in front of us and another terribly wounded; one having his head and neck cloven in two as if by an axe, as the shell burst close on them. Just as we got near Bouzincourt a bullet sang by, and well-aimed shrapnel burst very low over the village.

About two in the afternoon the shelling became extremely heavy, the shells bursting all around our underground shelter. The colonel called all the cooks and servants downstairs to shelter; the guard was wounded by a splinter from one of the shells and was brought down, his wound attended to and bound up. By a strange coincidence we found one shell had burst in exactly the same hole as a previous one by the side of the house. The walls quivered with the shock of the explosions, the fragments rattled down through the open gratings, and each shell seemed to fall closer to our shelter than the one before.

This tempest raged on until 6 o'clock, when it finally ceased. Cooks and servants reascended the narrow staircase and began to look around at the havoc the storm had wrought. Everywhere the roads were blocked with debris of the houses that had lined them, and we met some artillery officers who had come to see the damage. "We saw you were having a bad time, for the town was hidden by the dust of the falling buildings," they said, with which remark they took their way back to their batteries.

With that wonderful capacity for which army cooks are famous, a dinner was prepared in a wonderfully short interval. In spite of everything, there was soup and meat and two vegetables, and the cook apologised for the lack of " sweets " owing to the time being too short after the shelling to prepare them.

The next day, April 3rd, opened grey and oppressive, with rain falling at intervals. The rations were getting a little short, so the C.O. said : " I will reward any man who goes out and brings something back for the mess." Most of the headquarters men were speedily out in the village catching fowls, and any other live stock to be had, and thenceforth we had eggs and poultry in abundance—so much so that we were able to send round supplies to all the company messes.

The shelling continued with quiet intervals all the day. A party of the former inhabitants arrived to bring away some of their belongings and search for their money buried in the ground just outside the house. We went with them to the spot, and a heavy box containing their money was soon dug up and carried off, with many protestations of thanks for being allowed to come in. Then I had to go off with the guard to the other end of the village with another party. We had just entered the house when the enemy laid down a heavy barrage on the cross-roads on which the house was situated; the fragments and the dust of falling buildings made things a trifle unpleasant, and when the top story of the house fell in with a crash, we thought it safer to seek the shelter of the cellar, where we remained till things quietened down a bit.

The French owner, who had expressed his determination to remain under any circumstances, changed his mind, and the party left for safer quarters that night. One of their number was an old man of nearly ninety, and when I protested against their bringing this poor old man into such a dangerous situation, I was met with the response: "He is deaf and can't hear," which apparently was sufficient justification for taking him anywhere.

We got back to our cellar, and the rest of the day passed comparatively quietly. I visited Douglas in his aid post which he had established in a cellar not far away, and found some of our Catholic men and gave them Holy Communion.

The following day the rain fell without cessation in a perfect deluge, and we rarely ventured out of our underground shelter, which at least kept the rain off. That night we were relieved and made our way down through the intense darkness to Senlis. When we arrived there the rain had at last ceased, and we found a very comfortable billet in a good-sized brick-built house. I slept with Major Maynard and another officer on the first floor. Our valises were brought and we were able to undress and lie down in comparative comfort, an immense relief after sleeping in our clothes so long.

About 6 o'clock I was wakened by the major and told the place was being bombed. I got up half asleep and dressed to the unceasing crash, crash, crash! of shells bursting all around us. The morning was very misty, and at first I could not make out what was happening. It soon became clear we were not being bombed, but very heavily shelled, and this continued till about midday. One shell burst in the courtyard of the next house, killing one of our horses and wounding several men. Happily it fell in the midst of an immense manure heap, or the damage would have been much more serious. When the fog began to lift we were able to see the shells bursting just in front of us. The next day, Saturday, April 6th, I determined to say Mass, as my Communion case had arrived, so we used the very wide mantelshelf for an altar, and Sergeant Doherty and one or two other men received Holy Communion, and in the afternoon I carried the Blessed Sacrament to several of our boys in the neighbourhood.

Sunday morning we were able to say Mass in the same large room, and all the Catholics in the immediate neighbourhood managed to be present and received Holy Communion. The day passed very quietly, with hardly any shelling till towards evening. This night we were to move up to Bouzincourt again, and were forming up in the road getting ready to move up through the village when the enemy opened fire again. A shell struck the house opposite, killing one of the servants of the 15th, who were then just coming into the village to take over.

I remember I had committed the care of the battalion, and especially the H.Q.C., to Sister Teresa of Lisieux, asking her to take the company safely up to Bouzincourt and bring them out again unharmed.

As we got into the open country the shelling increased, the bursts always coming nearer. The darkness had fallen, only relieved by the frequent Verey lights sent up by the enemy. Just as we passed the cross-roads a shell approached with the loud, rapidly increasing roar that tells you it will either fall on you or else on one side or other of you. It burst with a tremendous crash just behind us. Showers of earth and stones beat down upon us. I called out: "Anyone hurt; is the Doc all right?" "All right; no one hurt." And so we went on towards Bouzincourt.

"The Lord has been good to us to-night," remarked the Doc quietly, just after the burst. It was a marvellous escape, seeing we had over sixty men moving all close together. Other shells fell fairly near, but after that we reached our old headquarters without any untoward incident. In the cellar once again we tried to sleep, but as the night was intensely cold, we only managed a fitful slumber, and were glad when morning came and the cook came round with the usual warming drink.

That very evening a shell burst in the mess of the field ambulance at Englebalmer, killing Captain Gaston and three sergeants and slightly wounding Captain Ironside. Captain Ironside, wounded himself, had to grope about and see to the wounded and dying in the darkness, not daring to use a light for fear of showing the direction to the enemy.

AT BOUZINCOURT

All Monday we worked hard strengthening our shelter by putting broken bricks, tiles, etc., to form a good bursting layer over the roof of the shelter. Colonel Parrish had gone down from Senlis to try and get some rest at Warloy, and so we had Major Maynard in command. We were only up for twenty-four hours and the whole day was misty and overcast, shelling in consequence not very heavy, although a good many gas shells were coming over.

The mist increased towards night and made the work of relief extremely difficult. The guides got lost and the hours sped on until towards 2 o'clock, when the relief, after wandering about in the darkness, had found themselves back again at the starting-point near the village. Lieutenant Brown went out and found them, set two companies on their way and took the other two up and brought our men down. He came in towards 4 o'clock in the morning, smothered from head to foot with mud, having fallen into shell-holes filled with mud and water in his efforts to get the relief completed. He had found the positions by the aid of his compass. He was utterly exhausted, and some hot drink was quickly prepared for him. We waited; another hour passed, but the companies he had set on their way had lost themselves. Out he set again and took them up to the line. At last, about 6 o'clock, the relief was finally completed, owing almost entirely to the devoted efforts of the lieutenant. We set off, together with the headquarters details, along the road to Hedauville, heavily gas-shelled all the way down, reaching the village at 8 o'clock, where a good breakfast set us up, and a sound sleep during the morning made us feel fit again.

The sun broke through the haze and everything took on a more cheerful air, although as we marched off in the afternoon to the point where the lorries and motor-buses were to meet us, we all looked something of a picture, covered with mud and dirt; yet the men were bright and cheerful, for we were going off for a good rest after weeks of hard and continuous fighting.

CHAPTER XII

IN THE TRENCHES BEFORE ALBERT

THAT afternoon we marched out of Hedauville to the point on the road where the buses awaited us, and we travelled thus the rest of the day and the best part of the night. Everywhere trenches were being hastily dug. At nightfall we arrived at what was supposed to be our destination, only to find the town occupied, through some mistake, by others. Our colonel expressed his views on the matter in language which adequately met the situation, and at least he secured the continued use of the buses for our tired troops. We wandered on, finally reaching a village where billets were available, and all got to sleep somewhere between 3 and 4 o'clock the following morning. That day the men rested, and spent their time in cleaning up generally, so getting back to something like civilisation again.

On Thursday, April 11th, we began our march to Francqueville, which we reached about 6 o'clock, after a hot tiring march. Everywhere as we passed the people looked at us with fearful and often with tear-stained faces, for the dread of the approaching foe was upon all. Carts, heavily laden with furniture, beside which old men and women tottered and children walked unrealisingly, the old people struggling along under impossible burdens, made up a sorrowful picture such as moved many of our men to tears.

When you entered a house, the poor people broke into such lamentations that conversation was impossible, and all efforts to comfort them were fruitless; and this met us all the way as we marched back towards the sea.

A night's rest at Francqueville, and early next day we began the march to Forest l'Abbé. The day was extremely fine, and we halted in the early afternoon and had lunch in a large field on the left of the road. The long march ended about 7 o'clock in the evening, and we settled down in the quiet tranquil country on the edge of the Forest of Cressy. Occasionally the low rumble of the guns could be heard in the distance, but most of the time no sound of war disturbed the placid quiet of the countryside.

The brigade was spread out in the various little villages scattered between Cauchy and Lamotte and Forest l'Abbé. Reinforcements began to arrive and battalions were brought up to strength. The rest and complete change of surroundings soon restored the troops, exhausted by the long struggle in which they had been engaged.

The people of the Somme, with few exceptions, never impressed us favourably; they rarely seemed to possess a soul for anything except money, and even removed the pump handles lest the troops should take water without paying for it. The men's impression of the people generally was summed up thus: "They are the meanest people I have ever met; they would not let you have the peelings of their potatoes if they could help it!"

From the religious point of view they were as a whole utterly indifferent, although there were a few villages to which this would not apply; but they were the exceptions that proved the rule. The churches wherever we went gave an impression of neglect and indifference, in striking contrast with what we had seen in Belgium and other parts of France.

On April 26th I went on special leave, reaching Boulogne the same evening and crossing to England the following day.

On my way back I went up to visit Father J. L. Bradley, who was acting as chaplain at the Canadian C.C.S. at Pernes. I stayed the night, and next day, by means of lorries, got as far as Canaples, where I lodged for the night at a farmhouse recommended by the Town Major.

I said Mass next morning in the village church and set out for the railhead, which was at Vernacourt, and from thence I jumped a lorry and arrived at Beaucourt, where I found the 4th Field Ambulance, and settled down for a couple of days. The first evening the enemy bombed the village and dropped one of his bombs through the church, smothering the whole place with fallen plaster and brickwork; however, my orderly managed to clear the sanctuary so that I was able to say Mass there.

I moved on to Warloy, as our brigade was settled in the banks and woods just behind the village, finding a lodging at the curé's house, and spent a few very pleasant days with one of the labour companies quartered in the town. The enemy planes raided us regularly every night, but fortunately comparatively little loss of life resulted, although a certain number of houses were destroyed.

The church, which was admirably kept, was well filled by our men and those of the other units in the neighbourhood. The men felt a special affection for this place where on the last Good Friday they had all received Holy Communion before going into action at Bouzincourt. The officers of the labour company gave every possible facility to their men to take advantage of the devotions in the church both weekdays and Sundays, and so every night we were assured of a number of fervent worshippers at Benediction.

After a short stay we moved to the village of Baizieux a short distance away. The brigade was distributed partly in the village and partly in the woods and camps between it and Franvillers. The enemy frequently shelled us with long-range guns, one shell descending into a tent, blowing it to shreds, and leaving a hole the exact size of the tent in the ground, while scraps of the officer's kit adorned the branches of the trees around. Curiously enough, the officer had previously lost all his kit during the retreat from the Somme, and had only just obtained his new valise, when this occurred. He had a narrow escape himself, having only left the tent a short time before.

Another morning the machine-gunners were badly caught in Baizieux, losing three killed and six wounded by a single shell which fell near their headquarters.

I had a wide front to look after, as we had two brigades in the line, and the months I passed on this front before Albert were some of the happiest and most consoling in my experience.

One day I took a long walk to the British cemetery at La Neuville, near Corbie, where one of our Earlsfield boys, Jack Foster, lay buried. The glorious spring day, the bright colours of wild flowers, made the little cemetery extremely beautiful and restful. I found the grave at last, and recited the *De profundis* for the boy who had fallen so bravely on the battle front only a few days after his return from leave. The guns were sounding all the time, strangely discordant with the splendid springtide glory of that day. On the way back I met some officers of the Australian Field Ambulance, who provided lunch in their mess, and we spent a very pleasant hour together. On June 1st I moved to the 5th Field Ambulance, just behind Franvillers, from which I could more easily visit the front line, which stretched across both sides of the Albert–Amiens Road.

Small raids were of frequent occurrence, and when orders came in from division, the C.O. would say to the adjutant, " Well, who had we better send for this job ? " and generally the answer was, " Smithers." So Captain Smithers would be rung up and appear : " Well, look here, Smithers, you have to make a raid to-morrow." " Yes, sir," said Smithers, and then the map and details of the operation would be discussed. Up to the very last, whenever there was any dangerous work to be done, Captain Smithers always led himself, and so was well loved and trusted by his men. " He *is* a soldier," they would say, and that is the best praise a man can receive.

My own brigade held the front on the right of the road, and the remaining brigade the front left of the road in front of Bresle. The whole country was alive with heavy artillery, especially along the Amiens–Albert Road. We had an advanced dressing station dug in on the right of the road, a short distance past Bresle, and another nearer the line on the left of the road close to the left brigade headquarters.

The whole front was fairly accessible in day-time, and all the battalion headquarters could be reached above ground, a great advantage, as it only occupied one-third of the time taken going through the trenches. Of course an occasional shell came over, and sometimes a short barrage would be laid down, which would delay one a little, but it was very different from the old days on the Ypres salient.

The rolling country of the Somme here was pleasantly broken by trees, for we were well back over the bare devastated land that stretched back for wellnigh twenty miles beyond. The spring flowers made the fields gay with colour, and the weather most of the time was gloriously fine, the long walks were extremely pleasant and exhilarating, and one lived out of doors from early morning till the long summer days closed in. The bursting shells in the midst of so much natural beauty seemed strangely out of harmony with their surroundings, yet strangely exhilarating.

One day I had sat down in a cornfield and was enjoying the song of the lark and the beauties of the field with the cornflowers and poppies, bright splashes of colour amidst the standing corn, when the shriek and bursting of a shell drew me back again to the actualities of war.

The early morning walks across the fields to the little village church in Franvillers, for Mass, and then back to our camp at the field ambulance, began the daily round. Sometimes I got a lift on the car up to the advanced dressing station on the Albert–Amiens Road, and thence a walk across the open to the battalion headquarters, and then the round of the trenches began. Generally the best part of a day was taken up with going the round of a single battalion; but the work was full of consolation and the troops extremely responsive. I tried as far as I could to let our boys have Communion once a week, for with two brigades in the line, and the artillery as well, more was not possible.

The Royal Welsh, too, had their position in the line, and numbered many excellent Catholics in the ranks; and then there were the machine-gunners' posts, where one was always welcome.

Alternate days I visited the various batteries, as often the men remained up with the guns for weeks or even months at a stretch, so their only chance of getting the Sacraments was for the priest to visit them.

One of the men of the Royal Welsh, Martin Corcoran, told me how he had seen in the church at Ribemont the sacred vestments and vessels lying scattered about. He hesitated to touch them, and then all through the night the thought of the sacred vessels left there kept coming back to him, and he felt he ought to have brought them away with him; so when he saw me coming up the trenches giving Holy Communion he was immensely relieved, and volunteered to come with me and carry back as much as he could. We went down to Ribemont, passing the sugar refinery, which was still burning, as it had been set on fire by enemy bombers the previous night, the charred carcasses of the horses making a ghastly sight, and on into the village and up to the church. At first I did not recognise the place as the same where we had spent our Christmas, so utterly changed did it appear. Most of the houses were wholly or partly demolished; the front of the one in which I had slept had been torn out, and the whole village was a scene of terrible desolation.

Within the church it was more pathetic still. One shell had brought down part of the roof of the nave; another had partially wrecked the sanctuary and sacristy. We picked our way over the debris, and set to work to select from the wreckage all that was worth salving. Corcoran had brought a large sack, and into it the vessels and vestments were all packed, and then we set on our way back. We kept above ground as far as possible, passing along the top of the trenches. I said to the Australians who were holding them: "I hope we shan't draw fire, walking along here." "We don't care if you do; we are leaving to-night," came the quick reply. This devoted soldier carried the heavy load after dark, right up to the dressing station on the Albert Road, whence it was forwarded to the Archbishop, who was then at Abbeville. The day after he went alone into the town, and under heavy fire rescued the remaining vestments, etc., that we were unable to move the day before. He told me what a privilege he felt it to have the opportunity of saving these church ornaments. I saw him often after, and he was always full of gratitude at these opportunities of receiving the Sacraments. He was wounded during our last days at Henencourt before the advance through Albert, and sent down to the base, and so I lost sight of him.

Another time I had a call to visit the field artillery who were in action in front of Ribemont. I passed through the railway station and part of Méricourt l'Abbé, now, like Ribemont, a mere wreck, its quaint little church badly shattered and most of the houses demolished.

I found the artillery just behind the ridge, and

one of the dugouts served for a little chapel, in which the men were able to receive the Sacraments; in fact, in these walks Communion was given in all sorts of odd places—one time in an observation post, next in a machine-gun post, again in the open trenches, or, as in the case of the Royal Welsh, in a large excavation, where all the men of a company were able to receive together.

From the front trenches one had a good view of the ground held by the enemy; we were just below the crown of the ridge on our side, the enemy just below on the other, and we could see Ville-sur-Ancre, just taken by the Australians, and the ridges held by the enemy beyond, with our shells breaking over them. Away in the distance was Morlancourt, which then seemed very far off. Little signs of life showed themselves by day, although there was a fair amount of activity by night.

On the whole our losses were remarkably small, but occasionally a big shell would get home and exact a rather heavy toll, as happened one morning, when the officers of the company in the front line were at lunch in their dugout, and a shell landed exactly on the dugout and brought it down in ruins, killing all the five officers who were in it. When they were finally dug out, one of them was still sitting back in the corner holding his knife and fork in hand.

It was during these days that I had my last conversation with Lieutenant Joseph Flanagan, one of our old St. Gregory's boys, and a splendid officer, who had the whole-hearted affection and devotion of all who served under him. I little thought, as we walked across the country to Franvillers, that it was the last occasion on which we should be together; but so it was, for he fell mortally wounded in the desperate fighting in Happy Valley in the month of August.

Our first turn in the trenches came to an end on June 18th, and on the day before I went to three labour companies in the woods behind Franvillers, where we gave Benediction in the open and had a large number of Communions.

About 2 o'clock one morning a head was pushed through the opening in our tent and a voice asked for the R.C. chaplain: one of our boys had been killed the day before, and they had just got his body down to the cemetery at Franvillers. The young soldier who came down for me was a friend of the dead man, and, knowing he was a Catholic, had come all the way from the line to tell me. I was up in a few minutes, and on my way back with him through the darkness, just relieved by occasional Verey lights and the flashes of the guns. In the cemetery, by the aid of a candle, I read the burial service, with the little group of men gathered round; the darkness and the continual roll of the guns added a peculiar solemnity to the last rites of the Church.

Just after we moved back to Saisseval district, delightful country, with all the scenes of war left far behind. We passed through Amiens *en route*, a city of the dead, silent and deserted, with all the houses shuttered and closed, here and there a building shattered by shell fire; but happily, although a great deal of destruction had been wrought, the cathedral and the greater part of the city escaped harm. Here, in the perfect weather and splendid surroundings, the division remained until July 12th, when we moved back once more into the line on the Albert front, but to the left of our old position, which now ran from the Albert–Amiens Road to the high ground close to Bouzincourt.

The time of our rest passed both quickly and pleasantly, and it was during this period that Padre Farebrother, the new Church of England chaplain, joined us, much liked by all the men, as he was an exceptionally earnest and tireless worker.

We marched from Saisseval and met our lorries at Ferrières, and travelled thence through Warloy to our camp on this side of the Henencourt Wood, situated on rising ground. The position was a very pleasant one affording a good view of the surrounding country, with some howitzer batteries close by, which somewhat annoyed the colonel.

The 21st were resting along the Senlis Road, so I walked through the wood to see them; coming back, I met a number of men working in the wood, whom I took to be a labour company, from the letters L.C., as I took it to be, but which in reality was L.G. I was on the point of saying: "What labour company are you?" but said instead: "Who are you?" and to my surprise received the answer: "We are the 2nd Life Guards." Fancy mistaking the Life Guards for a labour company! After a few days in the wood we moved back to Warloy, and I went to my old billet in the curé's house.

Our brigade went into the line on the left front, facing the Bouzincourt–Albert Road, on July 18th, and I went round the lines with the colonel the day following. The breastworks were rather low in the front trenches, but the day was a fairly quiet one, with very little artillery activity. For the first time we had a number of American troops with us in the line, in order to become acquainted with the methods of trench warfare. They were all very keen and interested, and as it happened largely Catholic. In a single trench I had over fifty Communions, and they all manifested the greatest eagerness to receive the Sacraments, so it was a great happiness to be able to minister to them. As the day was wearing on, I slept with Dr. Douglas in his dugout in the side of the hill, a point rather exposed to machine-gun fire, as I found out while shaving outside the following morning. Going up one morning, I met Mr. Connor's son from Wimbledon Park, who was doing motor driver's work in the flying corps, and our meeting so far from home was as pleasant as it was unexpected.

On July 23rd I moved up to the advanced dressing station, established in a part of the buildings belonging to the château, so as to be nearer the line, and gain more time for getting round the trenches. The 4th Field Ambulance was in the line, and Major Hughes in charge, with an American doctor for assistant. He was afterwards succeeded by Major Ironside, who remained up for the rest of the time. Our quarters were well protected with steel joists and several layers of sandbags, etc. And here I was able to fix up a little altar and say daily Mass for the first time in the line since my days up at Nieuport. On my way up one morning, as I passed the field artillery, one of the men said : " We are going to put down a barrage in a few minutes' time." I was glad of the information, as otherwise I should not have known what was happening.

The artillery opened out and lay down a heavy

smoke barrage on the whole enemy front on the right of the Albert–Amiens Road: it was an extraordinary sight; the whole front was rapidly hidden in one great screen of smoke, and under cover of the barrage the division on our right made their attack.

As I was watching from the side of the trench, the enemy began to open out, and shells were soon bursting all over the front, and they began to fall fairly close to us, especially on Murray Trench, where I was going my rounds. I met one of our old sergeants: " I am looking for my Catholic boys; are there any of them round here ? " " Yes," said he; " you will find them just round the corner, and they will be very glad to see *you*, Father." A little distance on I came on our boys, and as the sergeant had said, very glad they were to see the priest. The shells dropped close on the sides of the trench as they knelt, and the pieces were flying over our heads while they made their Communions.

Later in the afternoon I went along the front trenches: they had suffered badly, and for some distance were completely blown in. Fortunately, in spite of the heavy barrage, our casualties had been few, as the men had been drawn back from the trench in time.

On the left I found our old friends the machine-gunners, holding a series of posts just commanding the valley running down to Albert. From the lower part of the valley one had a very good view of the town into which our shells were dropping, sending up clouds of red dust from the falling buildings.

On my way across the fields I met two Americans, both Catholics, but one, for some reason or other, had never made his first Communion, and ever since he had joined up had been trying to do so, but without success. "Well," I said, "better make your first Communion now." So both knelt by the hedge and received Our Lord together. They were both profuse in their thanks as I left them. "Mother will rejoice," said the elder brother, "when she hears of this."

These days were intensely absorbing and full of consolation, as with very few exceptions the whole of the trenches up to the front line were accessible by day, which thus enabled all our Catholic boys to receive the Sacraments at as frequent intervals as I could manage to get round the very wide front we were holding. I often met General Gorringe making his tour of the lines, and I must relate one little incident, as it is so characteristic of him. He was standing up a little, looking over the top of the trench, when the guard near by said: "Beg your pardon, sir, there's a sniper over there. I was to warn you." As he spoke a bullet sang past the general, and then another. He remained for a minute or two, taking a good look round, and then stepped down into the trench. "Yes," he said, "it appears to be so; you had better warn everyone," and quietly went on his way.

In the early days of August we got the first rumours that the enemy was retiring along our front. The first impression was that he was only going back to draw us from our positions on the high ground before Albert, down to the mud of the river bank for the winter.

On August 8th we had occupied the railway cutting, and I went to visit our advanced posts, which were established in it. As I left our old lines and took the road up towards the railway cutting, there was a sense of something strangely uncanny as one walked along the silent road so recently vacated by the enemy. The German notices were still up in his old trenches, which had been a good deal knocked about by our fire, but he had an excellent series of dugouts, and in the railway cutting some quite good huts, filled with furniture taken from the town.

He filled a number of dugouts with gas and then chalked outside, as if by our own men, " Free from gas." Over some other dugouts was inscribed: " Bon Dugouts for the fat-headed Londoners"; while another legend ran : " Don't laugh, Tommy ; we are coming back."

From the opposite bank I had an excellent view, close at hand, of Albert, which I was not able to enter, as the enemy still retained his machine-gun posts in it. Albert was a heap of shattered brickwork, with a few houses in part standing. The great church was a shapeless mass, all the upper part of the tower being blown away, and the rest of it was blown up by the enemy a day or two later. Our artillery had been concentrated on the town with deadly effect, and often it has been entirely hidden by the clouds arising from the falling debris.

After seeing our boys and giving Communion, I turned back and met Major Maynard and some officers going up as I went down.

The next day or two Henencourt was heavily shelled, as the enemy used up all his ammunition before moving his guns back.

In a quiet interval I went to brigade headquarters.

The interval was very short, for just after I left there the enemy dropped a shell right into the brigade cookhouse and destroyed that night's dinner completely. This was on August 11th, and the next day we moved back to Warloy, and after a night there proceeded to Baizieux, where we spent two days before we began our advance.

The enemy front was now moving back along the whole line, and we were definitely leaving the long period of trench warfare for that of the open with its stir and movement, but under happier conditions than those of March and April.

This time up at Henencourt passed with wonderful rapidity; the long days out along the front and the pleasant evenings with Major Ironside in the mess at the dressing station will always remain with me as some of the best I have spent in the line.

CHAPTER XIII

THE GREAT ADVANCE

IT was a fine evening as we moved off, leaving Baizieux behind us, and clouds of dust rose as we tramped along the sandy way towards the Albert–Amiens Road. We crossed it a little this side of Bresle, moved down, passing through Ribemont, as night closed in, with the hum of enemy machines overhead, the searchlights playing fitfully across the sky trying to find them. The occasional crash of bombs dropping around sounded through the air as we made our way across the railway and through Méricourt l'Abbé, and after taking a wrong turning and marching in the direction of Ville-sur-Ancre, we got on the right track at last and arrived at our destination, a series of dugouts constructed in the bank of a valley midway between Méricourt and Morlancourt.

Colonel Parrish had left us shortly before we came out from the Albert front, and Major Maynard was in command with Captain Martin as adjutant.

The enemy had fallen back through Morlancourt, and was holding a position some distance beyond. The brigade was spread out, so that the 15th Battalion was in the forward trenches near the main Corbie Road, with the 21st away in the direction of Morlancourt, and our own men on the other side of the valley towards Méricourt l'Abbé, while the brigade and battalion headquarters were in the bank of the valley. During the ten days spent here our boys made their Communions in preparation for our going into the line. The evening of August 16th we went up to the lines in front of " Happy Valley," a position on the right of Morlancourt. We stood up on the top of the trenches looking towards the front; shells were coming over fairly fast on to the Corbie Road, along which we had to go; the August moon was shining fitfully through the clouds and giving a certain amount of light, while all along the front the flashes of guns and Verey lights showed on the horizon; the men were formed up in platoons awaiting the order to go forward.

It was about 9 o'clock when "A" Company moved up on to the road, the firing had died down, and the first part of the route was traversed without incident. When we left the road for the track, however, things became a little more lively and a few shells broke fairly close. We reached the road near headquarters, where we turned off to the left and got on the main road again. Just before we arrived one of the limbers had been caught by a shell, and as we drew near, I heard Captain Martin's voice coming out of the darkness: "Get away from this point quickly, it's d—— dangerous," although he remained himself until all had passed. We went on our way, and finally turned into the large disused brickfield on the left, amid which, in various shelters and dug-outs, our company was disposed.

The company headquarters consisted of a dugout with two entrances and four bunks, not intended for tall men; Lieutenant Carpenter and myself found them none too spacious, and besides, they had to serve the purpose of mess and office as well. The cooks did their work on the sides of the entrance to the dugout, and the signallers, etc., occupied the other, so we were all packed very tightly in our underground retreat. One curious effect of being underground is that, when a shell bursts, the vibrations coming through the earth give the impression it is ever so much nearer than it really is. We spent four days here, and in spite of cramped and restricted accommodation, the time passed pleasantly enough.

We were up fairly early next morning, and I had a request from one of our forward companies to go up and bury some enemy dead. I went forward and met Lieutenant Simmons and some other officers, and went to the wood where the German artillery had been making a stand. Both his guns had been shattered by our shell fire, and one of the artillerymen lay just as he had fallen, a ghastly blackened figure. "He was a brave man," said Simmons, regarding him thoughtfully; "he died at his gun." Poor Simmons, in a few days he too was to be numbered with the dead.

The wood had been shot to pieces, and only consisted of a series of upright scarred trunks, while the whole ground was pitted with shell-holes. In fact it was rather reminiscent of the old Passchendaele days. As on arrival it appeared another battalion was in charge of the burials, in order not to delay, I read the burial service for all the dead lying in the wood.

During these days we came across a number of dead, friend and foe alike, lying about, and little parties of our men were out all day digging graves for them. The heat had caused the bodies to decompose very rapidly; they were quite black, and in some cases we had just to slip a waterproof sheet under the body to hold the remains together. Anyhow, before we were relieved, all the dead in our area had been buried.

One day Lieutenant Carpenter and myself were

invited over to lunch to one of the companies in front of the wood. Just before we set out from the dugout the way there was heavily shelled, but we got across quite comfortably, and nothing fell very close.

The dugout was an old French one, and of course, conditions, as always on the front, were of primitive simplicity. That little lunch will always be remembered as the last at which I met two of our best and bravest officers, young Lieutenant Kent and Lieutenant Simmons; both were greatly loved by the men, indeed popular with everybody. We were all in excellent spirits, and enjoyed ourselves with the simple fare and surroundings, as somehow in the forward line we always did.

It seems strange that coming in from the most ghastly and sickening spectacles, with their grime, mud and blood, we could yet sit down and eat our meal so heartily, just as if nothing of the sort had ever crossed our vision.

And so, too, at night we fell asleep, quite undisturbed by the horrors that we had seen; indeed, I think that rarely, if ever, did the war intrude itself upon our dreams.

Certainly I have never slept better or more soundly than in the line, and somehow the monotonous crash of the shells very often helped to lull one to sleep; while the heavy atmosphere of the dugouts was conducive to slumber.

All the afternoon of the 20th, the night of which was to see our relief, was very lively, and shells fell continuously over the whole area around and behind the brickfield; indeed, things only quietened down just as we were moving out on to the road.

Captain Laird decided on keeping to the road, and as it happened we had a remarkably quiet journey down. We turned into a comfortless dugout for the night, full of creeping beasts innumerable, both great and small, and there was just a ridge in the hard clay floor, or rather in that share of it which fell to me, which proved more painful than pleasant, but anyhow we slept through it. I received orders to proceed at once and take on the advanced dressing station on the Corbie Road, in view of the attack on Happy Valley on the 22nd.

It was on this attack that Lieutenant Joseph Flanagan was killed. He was leading his men into the German position and had just exclaimed: " Don't kill them, take them prisoners ! " when he fell mortally wounded, struck in the lungs by a piece of shell. The man who had helped to carry him down came in wounded a day or two later, and from him I heard about Flanagan's last moments, and how, even in the stress of battle, his last thought was to save life and to spare.

I heard much from the men of his splendid and unselfish qualities ; when he had his parties of men out digging in, he took his share of digging himself, and so arranged the work that some might rest while others dug, and by his constant thoughtfulness for the men's welfare, was always sure of having their whole-hearted support. He remained conscious to the last, and had the consolation of receiving the Last Sacraments before he passed away.

We had the wounded streaming into the dressing station soon after 6 o'clock in the mornings of August 22nd and 24th ; mingled with our own men were many badly wounded German prisoners. The stretchers were lined up under a shelter and awning stretched over an open space at the side of the house that formed the dressing station. Most of our Catholic men were able to receive Holy Communion, as well as those amongst the enemy wounded.

It was in this fighting in Happy Valley, just at the close of the action, that Lieutenant Kent was killed by a bursting shell.

By Saturday evening the wounded had all passed down, and I went back to the 4th Ambulance at Querrieu and said Mass for the divisional troops there on the Sunday.

We were scarcely out of the line before we were moving back into it again, for after the hard fighting in Happy Valley the enemy was in full retreat, and so all available troops were pressed into the line to follow him up.

I got a car and went forward past our old A.D.S. and up the Corbie Road, passing the brickfield and the wood in front of it, and then turned off at the cross-roads to the right and on as far as the railway, which was as far forward as we considered it safe to take the car. Smashed guns, dead horses, lay about in all directions, as the enemy had only gone back some hours before. I walked back along the railway and found the 141st Brigade moving into their dugouts beside the line. The General and his staff had just settled into their shelter on the right of the line and were having an impromptu meal. They told me there was a Catholic in the 23rd Battalion near Fricourt who was wanting a priest, so I set off across-country in that direction. Shells were falling around some disabled Whippet tanks on the ridge, so we made a detour round them. I

THE GREAT ADVANCE

reached the battalion headquarters, an old German dugout in which they had just settled, very cramped but better than nothing. It looked as if it could be made much larger if some timber and galvanised iron at the back were removed, but we were suspicious of booby traps and let it alone. The man I was looking for was in the foremost company near Fricourt, so on again across the fields to a new line of trenches—old enemy dugouts, where at last I found my man.

I was just going to give him Holy Communion in the open trench as usual, but seeing he hesitated a little, I said: "Come under this shelter," a little corrugated iron affair at the side. Just as he was receiving Holy Communion a whiz-bang burst above us. It was well we came under shelter, for probably one or both of us would have caught some fragments if we had been in the open.

The artillery was fairly active along the front, especially just beyond Fricourt. I went back to battalion headquarters, where a welcome tea awaited us, then down into the valley and along the roads, where C.C.S. were already being hastily erected, through Meaulte, now reduced to a heap of ruins, back to our position in the old valley we had occupied before the advance.

Here Dr. Douglas left us, and I walked with him up the valley, past Morlancourt, to the field ambulance, which had just arrived at Meaulte, whence he was to take a car to his new appointment. He left us, regretted by all, as his very devoted work both in the line and out had been of much service to the sick and wounded of the battalion.

We remained here for two days, and on the last

day Colonel Kaye arrived to take command of the battalion. On the afternoon of Thursday, August 29th, we set off up the valley, passing through Ville-sur-Ancre, now little better than a heap of smashed brick and timber work; and leaving Meaulte on our left, we went forward in the direction of Maricourt. We passed an immense prisoners' cage on our left, with two Germans looking very much lost in its vast expanse; later we met seven more, coming down under guard to the same place. We passed some excellently constructed wooden huts in the chalet style, erected by the enemy since he overran the country in March, some of them quite artistic, with trellis-work and wide overhanging eaves.

Our series of huts were of the same type, well finished off, and fitted with simple but good furniture, and indeed were everything one could desire, although, of course, offering no shelter from shells or bombs. We had our dinner about half-past eight and soon after ten retired to rest, as we had to press forward again the following morning, the enemy being in retreat along the whole of our front.

The next day we rose at five and prepared to move into Hardecourt. We spread out in artillery formation, and so advanced across the fields on the left of Maricourt, towards the big timber dump. I saw a great part of the old corps rest camp had been destroyed, but the little wooden church in which I had said Mass last February was still standing.

As we were moving across past the old timber dump, a leave warrant came up for one of the men of our company. He turned back and set off to the rear in excellent spirits. We moved on and began to descend the valley, passing over 100 prisoners on their way down, and a number of dead Germans were lying where they had fallen by the roadside a few hours before.

Shells were falling fairly regularly on the opposite ridge, and our artillery was coming up and getting into position in the valley below. On the well-wooded Maricourt side of the valley the enemy had erected a considerable number of wooden villas, some of excellent design, on which a good deal of care had been bestowed. We made a long halt on the opposite side of the valley. A trench just behind what had once been Hardecourt ran along the top of the ridge. The village had disappeared completely, its site merely marked by a few tree stumps and a rather luxuriant growth of rank grass and nettles. We sat in the trenches and had lunch, with shells dropping over and sending up showers of dust and stones on our right.

I spent the afternoon in giving Communion to the machine-gunners, trench mortars, and the men of our own battalion; of eight men to whom I gave the Sacraments in a dugout on the hillside that day, only one came through unhurt in the subsequent fighting round Rancourt and Maurepas. I had tea with "B" Company in a large shell-hole, and going back, met Captain Smithers on his way up from leave. Late that afternoon we moved over the crest of the hill into some German-built huts on the other side. From this position we had a fine view of the whole battle front, reaching right up to the Bapaume-Péronne Road. Everywhere our guns were now pushing forward into action, and our observation balloons had followed us up and were close behind.

The enemy shells were breaking over the valleys and ridges along the whole front, and as evening fell the line was radiating with the electric-like flashes from the many guns in action. The ceaseless roll increased in intensity during the early part of the night, and became still more violent in the early hours of the following morning.

The next morning broke dull and grey, with just a sprinkle of rain falling. We buried eight men of the Royal Fusiliers in one grave, whom we found lying in various parts of our front. At 2 o'clock on Sunday morning the battalion moved up to the attack at Rancourt. I was asked to take the advanced dressing station early that morning in the valley on the right, as there was no priest there; so after the headquarters had moved off I lay down again for a few hours' sleep, and then went down to the dressing station.

Our attack on Rancourt had been a most complete success, and the losses comparatively light; unfortunately our new doctor, who had only just joined the battalion, was mortally wounded by a shell early in the morning and died soon after. The 15th and 21st suffered rather heavily. The wounded came down in large numbers and were lying in the open all round the sheds and shelters, under which as many as possible were placed. Many badly wounded Germans, brought down as the day wore on, added to the number. A considerable number of German prisoners were taken and employed on stretcher-bearing. The speed with which our wounded were got down was largely owing to their excellent work; all our men were loud in their praise of the work done by these prisoners. They were quite exhausted after their heavy task, and after being provided with food and drink were marched down the line. The day was very fine and helped to make the lot of our wounded lying out in the open more bearable. By nightfall, however, we had cleared the station and sent all the wounded down to the C.C.S. behind us. The enemy dropped some bombs across the road in the early part of the night, but the rest of it passed in comparative quiet.

On Monday morning, September 2nd, our battalion suffered heavily in the fighting before Moislains, owing to the failure of the division on our right. All the company commanders save one were killed or wounded, and many of the other officers as well. This morning, too, the wounded came down in large numbers.

The next day I went up through Maurepas, or rather the site of it (for except rank vegetation, there was nothing to indicate that the place had once been a village), towards Le Forest, another hamlet, as completely blotted out as Maurepas; just beyond it on the right I found our battalion and the 15th, resting after the strenuous time they had been through. Coming back at night, the Brigadier-General gave me a lift in his car, for which, as I had been on my feet the whole day, I was thankful.

On Wednesday I went up to Rancourt, the village we had recently captured, like the others, only a name for what had once been, and on the left of it I found the Royal Welsh in a series of trenches on the edge of the Bapaume-Péronne Road. It was a strange sensation standing again on that road, now absolutely bare of any sort of traffic, in striking contrast to the scene I had witnessed when I saw it in the midst of the March retreat. I was told enemy snipers were still abroad, and one had been caught the day before in Rancourt. I crossed the road and followed along the trenches on the other side and met an artillery officer, who told me he had walked forward several miles without seeing anything of the enemy. Artillery was fairly active; guns were being rushed up, and our howitzers were in action already not far from the road.

While waiting for a grave to be dug for three men who had been killed in the fighting on the 2nd, our Catholic boys came up to me to ask for Communion. It was singularly striking right out there in the open on the ground the enemy had only just vacated, to see our boys kneeling to receive their Lord, and very consoling to the priest to find them so eager in seeking the Sacraments. The officers of the Royal Welsh, as always, made me very welcome, and we had a pleasant lunch in the old trench dugout. The grave being prepared, I read the last rites over the boys who had fallen, and went back to the A.D.S. below Maurepas, meeting General Gorringe on the way. "Your parish is getting very extensive now," he remarked, as he passed on up the line. Thursday I went up to the Royal Welsh again to see to the burial of another man who had been found during the night.

By this time our guns had been brought close up to the road, and a great change had come over the scene. Lorries, cars, guns, and men were once more moving along it, and the road that had been silent and solitary the day before was now full of life and activity.

I went along to the hill on the right on which brigade headquarters had been established. Over the top of it I gained a striking view of the whole front, the smoke of battle rolling across in the failing light, and the red flashes of bursting shells made a striking and impressive picture. I came across several German dead lying amongst the bracken, and said the last prayers of the Church over them.

The wounded came in during Thursday night and early Friday morning in fairly large numbers. In the afternoon I walked down to the village of Cléry-sur-Somme, where the various transports were waiting to move off the following day, as we were finally coming out of the line that night. I shared a tent with two officers, and we were up early waiting for the lorries which never came. We waited till half-past two in the afternoon, and then determined to do the best we could for ourselves. We stopped a number of empty buses going back to Amiens and got a lift as far as Villers-Bretonneux. There we were stranded; there was no sign of traffic towards Corbie, through that shell-shattered town that had been the scene of some of the most bitter fighting of any in the Somme area.

There was nothing to do but tramp the intervening distance. After a long perspiring march we reached Corbie, and passing through Bonnay, finally arrived at Heilly just after darkness had fallen. We found battalion headquarters, and after dinner retired to rest after a very tiring day.

We spent Sunday in Heilly. We had the church (now badly damaged by shell fire) well filled at Mass, as another division was also in the town, and all present received Holy Communion. The Jesuit Father who heard confessions during the Mass was killed in action only a few days later. Amongst the boys who knelt at the altar rails was David Hooper, one of the old boys from home. It hardly seemed possible that one so young should be out with line troops, but so it was, and after Mass we had a long talk together over old times.

On Monday morning we set out for the railway station; we were leaving the Somme behind us, and going up into another sector of the front near La Bassée. We reached the station yard at a quarter to four, entraining was completed by 4 o'clock, and we set out for our long night journey, managing to sleep somehow in spite of the chilly air and the crowded state of the compartment. We arrived at Choques about 6.30 the following morning, and found ourselves fairly well placed for billets, although the village was in great part deserted, and a certain number of houses destroyed. It did not appear very inviting that sombre morning as we marched in through its muddy streets; rain had been falling most of the time; everything looked grey and cheerless, as it always does after a night of rain, but once we got into our billets and had been cheered by a good breakfast, things assumed a more rosy aspect.

CHAPTER XIV

SHOT AT DAWN

ON Wednesday afternoon I received an urgent call to go over to divisional headquarters at Labeuvrière; a side-car was waiting, and I was to take a few things for a night's stay there. No explanation as to why. I set off, and a quarter of an hour's run brought me up to the headquarters. Here I met our divisional chaplain and one of the staff, and found I was wanted to attend the last moments of one of the Catholic boys of the division who had just been sentenced to death, and was to be shot at dawn.

I saw the A.P.M., a kindly-hearted man who was really much distressed over the affair, as indeed I think everyone was; for there is an immense difference between seeing a number of men slain in battle and seeing one shot with all the cold deliberation that follows in such a case as this.

I saw the young soldier just after he had been brought to the place where he was to spend his last night. It was in one of the outbuildings of the old monastery. The grey Romanesque tower rose above the roofs of the monastic buildings, now all desolate and forsaken. The night was cold, with a driving rain, and Nature's mood seemed strangely in harmony with the sad drama in which I was to assist. The shelter was closed with a door of open ironwork; outside the guards were mounted with fixed bayonets.

The young soldier, for he was barely twenty, had joined the army on the outbreak of the War. He had more than once broken away from military discipline, overcome by an uncontrollable desire to wander. "It wasn't that I was afraid, Father," he said, speaking of his last exploit. " There was nothing to be afraid of ; there were no shells coming over." He was a little overcome with emotion when I saw him, as he had only just heard that his sentence was to be carried out the following morning.

He made his confession with great recollection. I gave him absolution, and then, kneeling on the bare stones, he received Our Lord with the most fervent devotion. We talked together some time, and as I was going away he said very earnestly, " Father, I am glad I am a Catholic, and I am not afraid to die." I promised to come back and see how he was later on, and if he was not asleep to see him again. About 11 o'clock I went back again; the clouds were scurrying across the sky, the wind sighing through the trees, and the rain beating down, as I went up the hill to the old monastery.

When I arrived the boy was asleep. I had just gone a few steps away, when one of the men came after me and told me he had just awakened. I went back and sat down beside him. He gave me a few instructions as to what he wished done, and I spent some time encouraging him for the fiery ordeal he would so soon pass through. The scene almost carried one back to the days of the martyrs, the boy was so wonderfully calm and resigned. No word of complaint. And he was full of confidence in God's loving-kindness and goodness.

I left him and went down to my billet and lay down in my clothes till about 4 o'clock, when I was called, together with the officer of the firing party, who was billeted with me, to go up for the final act of this moving tragedy.

The boy was awake and waiting my coming when

I arrived. The morning harmonised well with the surroundings, the wind moaning mournfully around the old building, the rain beating down pitilessly.

I entered, and he knelt to receive the last blessing and the Holy Viaticum, Our Lord coming to be his strength and stay in his passage from time to eternity.

I had prayed much to our little Sister Teresa to take the lad under her especial care and obtain for him strength and fortitude in his supreme need, and I was not disappointed.

We recited together the prayers for the dead, and continued speaking of the things of that world to which he was going so swiftly, until the tramp of the guard without announced the moment had come. The A.P.M. and the doctor entered. The boy did not wish to be blindfolded: "I shall not be afraid," he said to me. But he willingly submitted to it when he understood it was part of the regular formalities. His hands were pinioned behind him, and we were ready to move off. "Where is the priest?" he inquired. "Here I am, dear boy, just beside you," I said. The sharp word of command rang out, and the party moved off to the place of execution.

He walked with firm unfaltering step and took his place against the wall, while the firing party got in position before him. I stood beside him, we said the last prayers together, and then he repeated the threefold invocation of the Holy Name with great fervour. "Good-bye, Father," said the lad, as calmly as if leaving me outside the church after Mass on a Sunday morning. The quick word of command, and as I stepped aside, the rifles, blending perfectly, rang out on the morning air. His head fell forward on his breast. His soul had sped from time to eternity.

I stepped up and anointed him, the body still warm. The stretcher was brought up, the body rolled in blankets and carried to the ambulance near by, and in a few minutes we set out along the road to the little British cemetery, where his body was laid to rest with all the rites of Holy Church.

The boy's death and his fine courage made a great impression on all who assisted at that sorrowful scene, and bore striking testimony to the power of the Catholic religion in the most terrible circumstances.

I have never in the course of my experience assisted at a death more consoling or one in which I felt more absolute assurance of the state of the soul going forth to God.

Although I do not doubt his soul, through the merits of the Saviour's Blood, already enjoys the face-to-face vision of God in heaven, yet, mindful of human frailty, I beg the reader to have sometimes in prayerful remembrance the soul of this soldier boy who was shot at dawn.

CHAPTER XV

THE ADVANCE THROUGH LILLE AND TOURNAI

I WENT to Auchel later on in the day, where our brigade moved that morning, and met some of our headquarters men on the way there.

Auchel was a fairly prosperous mining village, with those great pyramids of slag about the mines characteristic of this district of France, the village itself reminding one somewhat of our Northern villages at home. It was untouched by the ravages of war, the people open-hearted and hospitable and the billets comfortable, and so altogether a welcome change from the desolate Somme area whence we had come.

The church was a spacious modern structure designed in the style of the thirteenth century, with a fine nave and aisles, well kept, open all day, and with a round of services excellently attended by a devout congregation. The church was packed at each of the four Masses on Sunday morning; quite a large congregation came together every night during the week for the evening devotions, and the parish reminded me of St. Gregory's at home, both in the arrangement of the services and in the interest the congregation took in the care of the church and sanctuary.

Here we passed our time very pleasantly for some weeks; the weather was fine for the most part, and the coming back to civilised surroundings made the stay very satisfactory to our boys. Towards the end of the time I was unexpectedly called to England, and went home via Calais, reaching London on September 27th.

I managed to get in a short visit to our Sisters

at Syon, and then spent a few days at St. Gregory's. I crossed to Calais on October 11th, and went up to the Church of the Sacred Heart, where I found Father Bodard. It was a pleasure to enter again this fine sanctuary, a centre of prayer and devotion, whose doors were always open from early morning till late at night. Benediction was just beginning when I arrived. The reverent demeanour of the worshippers, the recollection of the little band of altar-servers, manifest the care and devotion of the priests for their people, and how responsive the congregation to the care bestowed upon them.

After Benediction I went along with Father Bodard to the presbytery, where I met Sister Hilda, who was still working at the Anglo-Belgian Hospital, Sister Eileen having gone to work at one of the military hospitals in the South of France.

The next morning I rose early, said Mass at 5 o'clock, and after breakfast set out for the station at La Fontenelle. The train carried me as far as Berguette, which I reached about 11 o'clock. I learned that the divisional reception camp was about two miles away. As I wanted to get up to the battalion as quickly as possible, of course I avoided it, and looked for a car instead. I found one that carried me as far as St. Venant, and then picked up a lorry, which took me on to Lestrem. The driver happened to be a Catholic, and had been up in the Salient, so we exchanged our recollections of old times up there.

We passed through Merville, absolutely razed to the ground, with mounds of fallen brickwork on either side of the road. The handsome church was a thing of the past; it was a sorrowful contrast to the last occasion, when we had seen it all intact and looking bright and cheerful in the sunlight of early summer.

From Lestrem I walked along to La Gorgue, again a sad contrast to former days, for the church in which I said Mass at my previous visit was in ruins.

Along the road I met a young soldier, one of the old serving boys at Syon Abbey, in the years before the war. I was able to give him all the latest news from Chudleigh, and then set out to divisional headquarters, where, after lunch, I got a car on to brigade.

Our transport and stores were not far away, so I walked on and found them in some old German huts, just as darkness was falling, and was once more within sound of the music of the guns.

The next morning I walked up to Fromelles, where the battalion was in support, but coming out the following day; I was just in time to see Sergeant Doherty before he set out for England. On the way back I found the Royal Welsh and turned aside to see them, receiving, as always, a very warm welcome from all. We talked over the prospects of peace, and were all in cheerful and optimistic mood as to an early termination of the War.

Monday, October 14th, we marched off at 1 o'clock and, passing Lavantie on our right, reached Estaires in the early afternoon. It had been fired on the Germans retiring, so what the shells had spared the flames devoured, and all that was left of a large and prosperous town were blackened ruins and mounds of brickwork. We found a fairly good shelter at the edge of the village and spent the night there.

After the night's rest we moved on to a village just near the old front line, which we held after the spring retreat.

It was very much knocked about, but we found fairly good billets. We only made a day's stay and then marched to St. Hilaire, a quaint little village resting in quiet and peaceful surroundings, as the tide of war had stopped far away, and there was not even the distant sound of guns to disturb its tranquillity.

There was a most delightful little Flamboyant chapel near the château, and this we used for all our services, both weekdays and Sundays. On Saturday morning we rose early and I said Mass for the last time in the quaint old chapel. We moved off at 10.30 on our march to Berguette, which we reached soon after 1 o'clock, and then entrained for our journey towards the line. For a troop train we travelled very quickly, and soon found ourselves in the war area once more. We passed Bailleul, a ruined mass of shattered brickwork and masonry, and over shell-pocked country towards Armentières, of which we had a good view in passing. Not a house remained intact, and the whole city, like Bailleul, was one vast ruin ; a pitiful sight, made more pitiful as we beheld it with the sunshine playing upon its unutterable desolation.

Once past Armentières the country began to look less shell-stricken. On the way up Captain Martin had been cheerfully talking of dining in Lille, but, said the colonel, " I tell you there is neither food nor drink to be had there." So when we reached our detraining point and found another shelled village, the colonel turned to Martin and said,

"There's your restaurant, Martin"—pointing to a shattered restaurant at the angle of the road.

We swung off along the way paved with granite setts, and as we neared the suburbs of Lille the signs of civilisation became more abundant. We entered Lomme as the evening was closing in, and could just see the people lining the streets to welcome us, as with band playing we marched along the main road. It was a moving and inspiring moment, one not easily forgotten. We turned off towards one of the large factories that abound round Lille, imparting to it a Manchester-like appearance, and here the battalion halted for the night. The Germans had fitted up the factory admirably, a wooden bed for every man, with places around the iron columns for equipment, and chairs and tables. The factory was quite modern; built in 1912, the machinery of English make had not been completed when the tide of war swept over the city. The factory provided the finest billets our men had ever struck during the War.

A shadow of sadness was over every family, for the Germans in their retirement had carried off all the men and boys from the age of fifteen upwards. There were many stories of petty tyranny, of absurd regulations, and heavy fines for the most trivial offences. Food of a sort had not been wanting, but meat, eggs, and butter had been practically unobtainable, except to a very few, owing to the extraordinarily high prices demanded for them. The long years of anxiety, and absence of all outside news, rather than lack of food, had worn down the spirit of the inhabitants.

But they all welcomed us heartily, and our boys

gladly shared their rations with the people whenever they had need. The next day was Sunday, so I said Mass in the Church of the Sacred Heart at 10 o'clock, at which a large number of men of the two brigades assisted, and all made their Holy Communion in thanksgiving for the wonderful successes vouchsafed to us these days.

The parish Mass followed, and the spacious church, a fine modern example of Romanesque, was packed to overflowing. One noticed everywhere, mingled with the joy of deliverance, a sad, wistful look in the faces of the congregation; every family had at least one son missing who had been carried off into captivity, and fear for the fate of the loved ones mingled itself with the note of triumph, now the long-prayed-for day of victory had arrived. Next day, Monday, was fixed for the official entry of the British troops into Lille. I said Mass in the church at 7, and at 10.30 we set off along the main road into Lille. The weather was magnificent, the sun shone down from a cloudless sky, and nature rejoiced with us on this day, looked for so long, and which even recently had appeared as yet so far off.

The whole division, with the three brigades, transport, trench mortars, machine-gunners, and artillery, moved along the road with bands playing, and as soon as we had entered Lille, began to march at attention. As we passed through the opening in the ramparts, the band struck up the " Marseillaise," which was taken up by the voices of the onlookers with great enthusiasm. The march through Lille was a time that will always live in one's memory.

The way, with its cheering, sometimes weeping, multitude, simply overwhelmed with the great reality, the shouts of " Vive la France !" " Vivent les Anglais !" the flag-decked houses, the brilliant sunshine, all combined to make a scene that was intensely moving. Amongst the crowd I recognised some old pupils from the St. Bernard's Convent at Slough, carrying the mind back to days long before the shadow of the Great War fell upon the world.

The Grand Place was the culminating-point of the day. Here the pack of humanity had pressed through the barriers; on the grand stand was such an array of brass hats as we had never seen gathered together before. We reached the suburb of Fives, on the other side of Lille, in the early afternoon, where likewise we had a very enthusiastic welcome.

We were billeted in a fine château of the Victorian period, and soon got settled in. The neighbourhood of Fives was even more reminiscent of Manchester than the other side of Lille. I went out to find the church, which proved to be a very good specimen of the early period of the Gothic revival, with a lofty and spacious interior. I saw the curé and arranged to say Mass there at 7 o'clock the next morning. He told me a little of the sufferings of the civil population during the four years of German domination. Although there had been nothing like starvation, there had been many deaths owing to lack of nutrition ; but, as he said, the mental strain and anxiety, the absence of all information about relatives in the French Army, and the lack of intelligence from without, was far greater than the physical sufferings of that time. Several of the curés had been fined and punished for being too outspoken in their discourses, and there was always a representative of the German police to take note of whatever was said during public worship. The German troops themselves had been very short of food during the last days of the occupation.

Tuesday proved a fine day; the morning was bright and crisp, with just a touch of autumn in the air. There was a large congregation at the Mass at 7, and many Communions. During the morning I paid a visit to the 4th Field Ambulance, where we had lunch. The news of the capitulation of Austria, which had just come through, seemed to have a depressing effect in the mess, and, indeed, was taken rather in the nature of a disaster than a triumph; for one thing, Captain Tytler had neuralgia, which was certainly calculated to remove any undue optimism that the intelligence might give rise to, and the general opinion seemed to be that it would have no effect on the duration of the War. However, the major did his best to uphold the hope that Austria's going out must weaken the resistance of Germany.

On Wednesday, at half-past twelve, we formed up and moved off along the road to the forward area, and reached the village of Anstaing in the afternoon. The day was magnificent and the march a pleasant one. And so we entered the reserve line. What a contrast to former experiences of being in reserve! Here was a quiet little village, untouched by shot and shell, beds with white linen sheets to sleep in, and the people delighted to see us and eager to do anything possible for us. The houses were spotlessly clean, and there was no trace of war in this peaceful little spot.

The church was a very simple building with a

late Victorian tower in the classic style, and the rest of the building mostly in the style of the early Gothic revival, with an admixture of earlier work. The interior was spacious and not unpleasing, although the detail was poor and feeble.

The next morning when I entered the church, about 6.30, I was surprised to see such a large congregation: indeed, the majority of the inhabitants must have been present. I said Mass immediately, and gave Holy Communion to the Catholics of the headquarters company. We heard news of the extremely quiet front to which we were going; civilians living in the lines and in No Man's Land, so we looked forward to quite a picnic. At a quarter past twelve we moved off across-country, and on the way up met the 21st at Cornet, where we halted to wait for guides.

As we entered Blandain we came once more upon the familiar evidences of war. A good many buildings had been damaged by shell fire, and after we had passed through the village some 5·9 shells began falling over on our line of route. One fell just in front, and an artillery officer came out from a house on the right and advised us to move off to the left, so as to avoid the cross-roads, which we did. As a matter of fact that was the last shell to come over that afternoon.

We reached our new billet as night was closing in, a fine well-built farm, in Honnevain, where the headquarters of the battalion we were relieving awaited our arrival. Here I met Father Devas, a Franciscan Father, and brother of Father Devas, S. J. We learned that our position was not quite so peaceful as we had been led to expect, as a shell had fallen the previous evening and blown in the windows. The weather had become overcast, and a drizzling rain was falling, which made the shelter of the farm-house very acceptable. We stood on the doorstep talking over things and our prospective return once again to the ordinary round of religious life, until the relief was complete.

Most of us slept in the large room next the street, and the colonel, the adjutant, and Major Feron occupied the three rooms farther along on the same side of the house. We were all pretty tired. While some sat up until midnight, in case the enemy should shell again, the rest of us retired early and got a good night's sleep, rudely broken about 3 o'clock the following morning by a shower of high explosive shells, which fell on the road and around the building. I heard a voice out of the darkness saying: " I'm out of this." So very soon we all dressed, and before our heads were fairly out of bed we had caught a dose of gas, which poured in through the broken windows. We made our ways to the mess, coughing and spluttering, with eyes and noses running, and feeling just a little sorry for ourselves. The doctor quickly got ready a solution of carbonate of soda, which eased our discomfort somewhat, and then the cook brought in some hot tea. Meanwhile, the shelling having died down, we got back to our beds and had a good sleep until about 9 o'clock. It was curious that this shelling occurred just after a wire had come through announcing an armistice with Austria-Hungary and Turkey.

At breakfast the desirability of arranging another billet was discussed. As Captain Martin expressed it, the place was "too d——d dangerous; it's plump in the line of fire, and they can't help hitting it." I went over with Lieutenant Eaitch to see if the little château over the way would prove more safe. A shell-hole in the wall and a 5·9 shell-hole before the door suggested that there was little to choose between it and our present surroundings. I little thought this was to be our last walk together, and that within a few hours he would have passed out of this world. The doctor and myself went up to see one of the Belgians recently gassed. We found the family living in a well-constructed German dugout, brick-built, with a very thick concrete roof, as they had abandoned their farm-house opposite after it had been struck by a shell.

This afternoon the Mass set, to replace that lost during the advance, arrived, so I was able to arrange to say the three Masses on All Souls' Day in the large room of the château.

We mostly retired early to bed, but Lieutenant Eaitch remained writing a long series of letters to all his friends at home; indeed, I never remember his having spent so long a time or written so many letters before. Had he any presentiment of what was coming? If so, he gave no sign, for he was just as bright and cheerful as usual.

I slept well until about 5 o'clock, when our guns put down a very heavy barrage. Towards 6 o'clock we could hear, amidst the ceaseless din of our own guns, the sharp crash of enemy shells falling near us.

Soon after I heard the rattle of the gas guard going, and someone entered and called Lieutenant Eaitch, telling him that gas was about. A little later he came over to me and said, "Lend me your torch for a few moments"; those were the last words I heard him utter. Just after he went out there was a violent crash as a shell struck the building, followed by the sound of falling glass. I heard Captain Martin's voice, and we got out of bed, to find the corridor full of dust from falling debris. We made our way to the end room, occupied by Major Feron. As we got near we heard his voice from within: "Martin, what is all this d——d row about?" We pushed in the door, found the front wall blown in, the room strewn with brickwork and wreckage, and the major still in bed under a pile of smashed timber and broken bricks, and quite unhurt. It was indeed a miraculous escape. Meanwhile, we heard an officer had been hit, and we made our way to the entrance gateway, where the doctor was already binding up Lieutenant Eaitch's wounds. He had been struck by pieces of the same shell in both lungs, and had fallen to the ground directly he was struck. He was unable to speak and was breathing with great difficulty. A wheeled stretcher was quickly procured, and he was taken with all speed to the A.D.S., but, alas, he died soon after his arrival there. So passed away one of the bravest and most well beloved of the younger officers in the battalion. Whoever came in contact with him appreciated his never-failing cheerfulness under the most adverse circumstances. He was admired and loved by the men, and to say that is to pay the highest tribute possible to an officer. His passing cast a shadow over the mess, and left a strange sense of vacancy; indeed, it seemed hardly possible to believe his happy, cheery presence had gone from us for ever. On this same day the news came through that Major Maynard had died in England soon after he had arrived at Netley Hospital.

At 9.30 I said the three black Masses in the large room of the château, which made a very good chapel. All the Belgian people in the neighbourhood came, young and old, and were full of delight at the opportunity of hearing Mass again. Our Catholic boys around were present too, and received Holy Communion. The Masses were said to the music of bursting shells most of the time. The rest of the day was fairly quiet, as was the night also. During the afternoon the mess and some of the billets were moved to a house farther up the road.

Sunday was a fine day, and Mass was said in the château; again extraordinarily well attended—even the children came. A shell burst on the crossroads, and some others near by, while the Mass was being said. Happily all got safely home again. All day long a stream of poor people evacuated from the front line passed along the roads, our boys helping the poor old people and children along, carrying their bundles and wheeling carts filled with their belongings, the whole of which had to be brought down by hand labour, as the Germans had removed all the horses when they made their retreat. It was a pathetic sight to see this stream of sad-eyed people moving down, amongst them some forty nuns of the *Sainte Union* Convent; some of them, over eighty years of age, had to be brought down on stretchers.

Later in the evening more sisters arrived, sent down by the 15th, five from the Convent of the Assumption, and three from the Convent of St. Teresa.

The colonel provided tea for them, and also dinner, which the cooks readily prepared, pleased to do anything to lighten the discomfort and suffering of the refugees. We had also a poor girl suffering from influenza, and her little brother and mother. Those who could go were sent down by the ambulance, and the rest were sheltered in the château for the night.

Monday proved an extremely fine day, a little fresh, with brilliant sunshine, which gave the enemy very good observation, as we soon found out. I said Mass again in the château, where we had a large congregation. Afterwards we were called to the sick girl up the road in the dugout, and the doctor decided to send her down by ambulance to Lille.

The enemy began to range round, dropping shells promiscuously in all directions. Three spare pieces came singing past, very close over one's head, near the cross-roads.

At 2 o'clock the advanced party set off up the road, and we reached our headquarters in Froyennes, a fair-sized house on the main road to Tournai, about 3 o'clock.

I went round to the Dominican convent, where the sisters were still remaining. They were overjoyed at seeing a priest, as they had been praying all day that a priest might come.

The convent proper was a quaint old seventeenth-century building, forming a quadrangle, with a chapel, which had had a couple of shells through it. I found the sisters all prepared to leave, as they had been warned to do so, but naturally they desired to cling to their convent home. " You do not wish to leave ? " I said to the Superior. " Well, no, we do not," she answered. " Well, stay here, and do not trouble; I put this house under the protection of Sister Teresa of Lisieux and the house will not be touched." And with a promise to return and say Mass in the morning I left them. I went up the road to our trench mortar battery, where to my surprise I found an English family who had been living there for twelve years. It was a pleasant meeting, particularly as I knew some of their friends. I dined that night at the trench mortars' mess. In the midst of dinner a very heavy barrage of artillery and trench mortars, to the accompaniment of machine-gun fire, broke in upon our peaceful repast. Some bullets from enemy machine-guns were passing over the house. It lasted for the best part of an hour and then slowly died down. We found out later that two of our posts had been heavily attacked, but had successfully beaten off the attack, and suffered only one casualty. I said to myself, " Well, the nuns won't think much of the first night of Sister Teresa's protection."

The stars were shining brightly as I went off down to our headquarters, the machine-guns still busy and occasional shells dropping over; but soon after I got in all became quiet again. One of the enemy shells had blown in the windows of our quarters, which gave us more ventilation than was strictly necessary.

Next morning I went to the convent and said Mass for the sisters in the temporary chapel. The whole area was heavily shelled, and one gun persistently dropped a shell outside in the garden every few minutes during Mass, and so I had to wait a litlet before I left the convent till the noise quieted down a bit; the convent itself was never touched. During the day we had the news of the terms of the Austrian armistice, which cheered us immensely. The doctor became quite optimistic, and quite changed his opinion "that this War is never going to end." A heavy shelling during the morning showed that at any rate the War was still on.

To-day it was comparatively quiet and the General looked in and told us our armistice terms had been published, and *The Times* correspondent said they would be immediately accepted. However, a few shells are still flying about, so evidently the armistice has not yet begun.

We must not omit the story of two members of the Belgian Mission, who had been sent up to evacuate the civilians. As soon as they had sent the people down towards the rear and turned to get others out, they found the first evacuated had slipped back to their houses again.

"These Belgian officers are no good," said the 15th Battalion, when we came up for relief; "they simply worry round us here for rations." I wondered why the two officers looked so glum, but we found out that they had been practically without any food for two days, so that it was not altogether surprising. Between that, and their inability to get the people away, they were very sick of their job, not to mention much annoyed. However, we arranged to feed them, so all was well that ended well, but despite this they went off just afterwards in great disgust.

And here we are, waiting for the fateful news to come through. There is only one wire that has any great interest for us now : " Germany has signed an armistice which will be effective from . . ."

" What a life ! I don't think this War ought to be allowed." It is Martin's voice, but still he is very optimistic, as we all are, and are just waiting for the last word. It is indeed a great thing to have lived to see these days.

CHAPTER XVI

HOW THE END CAME ON THE WESTERN FRONT

WEDNESDAY evening we got the news through on the wire of the terms to Germany, and we all felt that the days of peace were not far off.

Nevertheless, the night was by no means quiet, as the house was heavily shelled, and the crashes of falling brickwork and broken glass told us that some of the shells had got home. However, after the final shower the rest of the night was comparatively quiet.

The Brigadier-General sent a characteristic wire inviting me to spend a few days with him : " To Fairly Reverend Happy Days.—Will you come to-morrow and stop with us for a few days ?—General Kennedy."

Next day I said Mass for the Dominican sisters in the convent at 8 o'clock, and afterwards visited "A" Company, whose headquarters were in the convent of the *Sainte Union* sisters. At 2 o'clock in the afternoon we set out to go down to the brigade headquarters at Cazeau, calling in on the way to give one of our boys Holy Communion.

We had just got clear of Froyennes when the first shell came over, and after that a fairly heavy barrage commenced. As we rightly guessed, the enemy was firing off all his ammunition before moving his guns back; we turned left along the railway, and the shelling became more intense, the splinters falling all around us. Indeed, for about twenty minutes it was as lively as anything we ever experienced in the old days at Ypres. We got cover at last in a large hole blown by a mine, and waited till the shelling quieted down a little, and then got on to the farm-house in which we had stayed at Honnevain. Here we had a warm welcome from the family, and after coffee and a short rest set out along the Templeuve Road. Shells followed us all along the way till we reached the village. That was our last experience of being under fire, and, indeed, the close of the enemy artillery activity on our Front.

We reached brigade in time for tea, and had one of the best and quietest nights' rest for a long time.

During the night the news came through that the German delegates had crossed our lines and gone to General Foch's headquarters. The morning was singularly calm, not a sound of artillery activity along the whole Front. I walked over to the 15th Battalion, whose headquarters at Cornet were established in a most interesting old sixteenth-century house, with several vaulted chambers and some very handsome chimney-corners. Coming back I lost the direction, and finally reached Templeuve and turned into the 5th Field Ambulance, where Captain Millar provided lunch.

Early in the morning some of the inhabitants of Tournai reached our lines and told us that the enemy had evacuated the eastern part of the city.

Our patrols went out towards the river, but found the enemy still held the opposite bank with machine-gun posts. Six of our men were killed and five wounded, the last casualties of the war on our Front.

I first learned what had happened from two of our wounded, who had just been brought down to the dressing station. The day was a wretched one, with a steady rain, and I was glad to get back to the shelter of headquarters. Here the wire told us that the enemy had till 11 o'clock Monday to decide whether to accept or refuse the armistice.

Saturday morning our planes, flying low over Tournai, found the whole city *en fête* decorated with flags, and the people crowding the streets.

The orders to cross the Scheldt were given, and the pontoon bridges were quickly put over the river by the engineers. I walked out to Froyennes, and arrived just in time to see the colonel and adjutant going forward. Civilians coming back reported the enemy in rapid retreat, and already a considerable way back. Brigade moved forward in the afternoon, and after a short halt at the White Château, formerly the headquarters of Prince Ruprecht, moved across the Scheldt. The sun was setting, and the quiet tranquillity of the autumn evening was in striking contrast to the stream of limbers and waggons struggling across the narrow pontoon bridges over the river.

We settled for the night in a very pleasant house, where we all had excellent beds and abundance of accommodation. The large dining-room was very chill and cold. In one corner was a large glazed-brick heating apparatus, erected only a few weeks before by the Germans. It only began adequately to warm the place by the time we were going to bed, and the only way to get warm was to stand with one's back flat against the side of the curious erection.

On the way I looked in at the church at Blandain. A shell had come through the roof and filled the church with fallen plaster, etc., but a number of our boys were hard at work helping the poor old caretaker to clean it out for Mass on the following day.

Next morning, the historic day on which the armistice was signed, opened cold and brilliantly fine. I went across the road and said Mass early at the Ursuline convent, and then went back to the White Château at Froyennes, to bury our poor boys killed in the last fight of the war. It was strangely pathetic and moving to look at the white upturned faces that one had seen in full vigour of life so short a while before.

Some artillerymen helped to carry them to the grave which the men of the 15th Battalion had dug for them the night before. I then set off along the road after the brigade. Everywhere people were out, overjoyed at their deliverance. Some handed flowers to the boys as they passed, others handed out coffee. Everywhere the note of joy, gladness, and relief at the great deliverance filled the hearts of the people. Along the road streamed back the men and boys who had been carried away prisoners by the enemy, and abandoned in his retreat. They carried flags, sang the "Marseillaise," and toiled along determined not to rest until they reached their home at Lille. They were of every age, from mere children to old men, just able to struggle along, but all were glad the enemy was crushed, the net was broken and they were delivered. "You are our deliverers, you are our saviours." These were the greetings as we went forward along the road. As I was passing through Quartes, the curé met me and said: "Father, you are tired; come in and rest." I was feeling a little spent, having been on the road since 9 o'clock, and it was now half-past three. A bowl of hot milk and two eggs came in very acceptably. Here I learned that a howitzer battery only left at 10 o'clock the previous night. Our advanced post reached Melles, only a mile away, and suddenly the word passed that the English were approaching, and the guns were quickly under way. That was the last the curé saw of the Germans, and at 6.30 next morning, as he was on his way to early Mass, he saw the first English soldiers entering the village. " For four years we have led the life of slaves," said the curé, " and you are our deliverers." The curé accompanied me part of the way, and as the darkness was falling I reached Barberie, the village in which the brigade had halted. It was the last night of the War.

All the arrangements had been made for continuing the advance in the morning, when just as dinner was over orders came to countermand the move, and instead we were to return to La Tombe. We passed some unexploded mines with a certain amount of anxiety, after we had seen two go up behind us. Next morning, Monday, November 11th, we moved off on our way back, passing the 74th Division hastening up to take over our front. We had not got very far when an aeroplane, flying very low and covered with streamers, passed over us, the first indication that hostilities had ceased. A little later the news spread along the battalion that the armistice had been signed on Sunday, and that at 11 o'clock the shadow of the great conflict had lifted. Victory triumphant and complete, and peace, had come to us on the Western Front. Strange to say, there was no sign of triumph. The succession of swift-moving sensations through which we had passed the last few days had, perhaps, dulled our senses. There was only a sigh of relief that at last the strife was ended. We reached our halting-place, and the men dispersed to their billets.

That night a solemn hush seemed to fall upon all. The great and overwhelming triumph caused no such hysterical and foolish outburst as that which disfigured the night at home, and utterly disgusted all at the Front who heard of it.

As one of our sergeants, on leave at the time, said: "All the row was made by soldiers who had never been out at the Front, and munition workers who were so annoyed at losing their soft jobs they were ready to destroy anything." The men who had been through all the cruel reality of war only felt a strange sense of solemnity, and their minds turned back to their comrades who had fallen; indeed, when we reflected on the tremendous price that had been paid to win peace, none of us could spend these hours in senseless and noisy rejoicings.

As I went round to billet after billet it was always the same—a sober restraint, and the memory of the boys who had gone was uppermost in everyone's thoughts. And so in sober quiet the great night was kept along the Battle Front.

The next morning I said the Mass of Thanksgiving in the convent of the Redemptorist nuns, and afterwards we sang the *Te Deum* in thanksgiving: "This is the day which the Lord hath made; let us be glad and rejoice in it."

* * *

The day so eagerly and long looked for has come and gone, and even out here we can scarcely believe, much less realise, that the awful nightmare has really passed, and that the shriek of the shell and the rattle of the machine-gun will be heard no more. The front line no longer exists; there is no going up to the trenches: all that is passed away as if it had never been.

In Tournai on Friday morning the whole city streamed into the great cathedral to give thanks to God for the great deliverance. The first strains of the *Te Deum* rang out from the choir as I entered by the transept door. The whole church and triforium galleries were packed with one solid mass of humanity, while down the centre of the church the Belgian troops kept an open passage.

Surely the grey walls of this old Romanesque church have never in all their long history looked down on a ceremony so moving as that of this morning. The great hymn associated with so many occasions of rejoicing through the ages once again expressed all the emotions of that great throng with a completeness that nothing else could, and brought the triumphant joy of to-day into union with all the joys of the past.

The last prayers are done, the great organ crashes forth, and the procession moves down through the great rood screen to the western doors. The acolytes, brilliant in scarlet and white, give a splash of colour in the midst of the sombreness of the serried mass through which they make their way. The bishop in cope and mitre, with joyful, smiling face, raises his hand in blessing right and left as he passes.

Then stream out behind him Ministers of State, the city fathers, generals—Belgian, English, and

French (but the English predominate)—and the great act of thanksgiving is done. The Belgian national anthem crashes from the organ, and is taken up by the throats of thousands, eyes overfilled with tears of joy—Belgium is free once more.

After I make my way to the 4th London Field Ambulance, where the crowds of released prisoners are being cared for. Thousands have streamed down, English, French, and, when I reached the hospital, Italians, all overjoyed at their deliverance, and already beginning to forget their past miseries in the joy of the present happiness. Released civilians tore along, bearing the burden of all their belongings on their backs, seemingly oblivious to fatigue, their one desire being to press on and reach their homes and families at the earliest possible moment.

And Nature herself rejoices with us, for the sun has shone brilliantly from a cloudless sky ever since that fateful hour on Monday last, when the strife of battle ceased on the Western Front.

CHAPTER XVII

AFTERWARDS

AND now we are back in the old area of Auchel, waiting, waiting—to go home. How long will it be?—we have no idea, for the cumbrous demobilisation scheme that has been set in motion moves very slowly—painfully so for us waiting and longing to be home; and the whole scheme, so far as we can see, seems to be more concerned with providing soft jobs for those who, having had them all through the War, seem destined to have them for evermore, than anything else. And we feel that our own orderly room is easily capable of arranging the whole business in a hundredth part of the time, with no extra cost whatever; and yet we must wade through the sea of useless forms that officialdom uses to release even a single man.

A letter direct to the C.O. from the employer of the man wanted, stating when, wages paid before the war and to be paid now, and the whole of those who have their work waiting for them could be on their way home, instead of being strangled with red tape. There would remain the men who wish to join the regular army, and those wanting employment, and these, too, could all be dealt with in much the same way. But, of course, anything so simple and direct is out of the question. There would be too many soft jobs missing.

The strenuous days in France and Flanders are over, and at lunch and dinner we talk over past experiences and live the stirring scenes of the past over again.

We left La Tombe, with its great and historic memories, behind us regretfully, for there we had experienced our first days of peace, and been warmly received and welcomed by a grateful people. Carbonnell had brought out his silver, long buried, and gave to our mess in his fine house quite the feeling of home, and when Madame returned from Brussels this was complete.

Then, too, just across the road, was the beautiful chapel of the Redemptoristine nuns, where the voices of the sisters had rung out the strains of the *Te Deum* so triumphantly, and all things around seemed to share in the great gladness of that wonderful time.

From La Tombe we marched back over the railway by Tournai station, back through Froyennes, Honnevane and Blandain to Willems, where after a short stay we began our march past Lille to Haubourdin. On the way we halted for lunch and went to a little cottage where our meal was served. One of the party made some remark about the house needing repair: " After the war is over," said the young girl quickly. " But it's over now," we said. " Oh, no, it isn't," said she. " When the English go home and the French come back, *then* the war will be over." She gave utterance to that which many people were feeling, but did not care to express so frankly.

The next day our way lay across the desolate battle area, which we were to see for the last time. It was a long march, nearly twenty-three miles, and a good test of the endurance of the troops. We moved off at 8 o'clock, reaching La Bassée, so famous in the story of the War, about 12 o'clock. Of course the whole town was razed to the ground, and as we passed we saw a few of the former inhabitants, who had returned, searching amongst the ruins of their old homes, in the hope of finding something to save from the wreckage. We reached Ginchy and halted near the brickstacks, the scene of some of the bitterest struggles of the War, and had our lunch in the open. Some boxes of ammunition provided table and chairs, and we sat down to our meal in this old war area, now strangely silent, but surrounded on every side with signs of the surging tide of battle that had swept over it so often.

It was dark when we reached Fouquereuil, and the brightly-lit mess with its blazing fire was both cheery and welcome. After a night's rest we moved off next day through Auchel to Cauchy, and here we seem likely to remain till the moment comes for us to cross the seas to the dear land at home.

And our mind reverts constantly to the past, to the days so full and stirring, when life and death were such near neighbours, days that, despite all their horror and misery, were supremely happy days, happy because of the splendid spirit of comradeship which the combined suffering and danger of the Battle Front impart so quickly, the helpfulness, the selflessness, the thoughtfulness, that compensated for a thousand discomforts.

And the spiritual joy and consolation of the priest, in those long tramps across the open and through the trenches, bearing our Blessed Lord to His children; their responsiveness and joy at His coming; the sense of exhilaration stirred by the occasional shell, sometimes, as on the Somme, seeming so out of place, amidst the glorious sunshine and the cornfields, bright with the scarlet of the poppies and the glorious blue of cornflowers; or as in the Salient, the long solitary tramps along unending duckboards in the half-light, through the great brown crater fields, and the search for our Catholic boys in the shell craters in which they were established—it is all a glorious and inspiring memory that can never fade away.

And, it may be said, what of the effect of the War on the boys; of what are they thinking; what of the spiritual influence of the War?

Well, from a fairly wide experience of the Front, from the sea to the Somme, one can say that, as far as Catholics are concerned, the occasion has afforded the opportunity for the return of many to the practice of their religion after long years of neglect, and it has been embraced gladly. Indeed, I can only recall a single instance where the opportunity was not taken. The gratitude of the boys, their fervent "God bless you, Father!" made up a hundredfold for whatever suffering and discomfort had to be endured in the effort to reach them.

Going through the trenches up at Nieuport, I remember hearing one of the non-Catholic boys, just after I had passed, exclaim: "God bless him and take care of him!"—and the non-Catholics were ever ready to let their Catholic comrades know when the priest was about: One of the runners, just before that terrible night at Nieuport, went on in front of me to call the Catholics as I came along; it was the last time I saw him alive, as he was one of those killed that night. The men who have looked death in the eyes, not once but many times, cannot return home and leave the impression of those great days behind them.

What are their feelings towards the enemy? Very different from those of the people who have never left the security of the homeland. During all my experience on the Front, even when the enemy was raining his shells on us, I have never heard an expression of hatred uttered by our boys. "Poor old Fritz has got up with a sore head this morning," they will say when a most unpleasantly heavy shower of shells has arrived in the morning out of the usual time; or, "Poor old Fritz is getting it just the same"; or, when our own fire was very heavy, "I'm sorry for poor old Fritz, he's having a rough time." That is the spirit of the English soldier all through; it is expressed by Bairnsfather perhaps better than by anyone else. He takes things just as they come, bears no malice in his heart, and is a striking contrast to the fire-eating people at home, who have never smelt powder of a more dangerous kind than that of the 5th of November. He is only amused at what he reads, retains his own point of view still, and does not take it from his instructors in the Press. "After all," he says, "the German mother sorrows for her boy just like ours." Such is his point of view of the War. Who shall declare his wonderful patience and endurance in the midst of the most utter misery, for the mud and misery of the trenches often impress far more than the shells? No words can convey, to those who have not seen, what the soldier boys—I had almost said children—have endured, with such magnificent spirit and courage, on that far-flung battle line of the Western Front, through those long-drawn-out years of conflict. His unselfishness and readiness to share whatever he has with his comrades, his gentleness and tenderness to the wounded, his contempt of danger when it is the case of carrying out an order or saving a comrade; his calmness in dark days, as on the Somme, when machine-gunned out of one position, he falls back on others and sights his rifle again as if nothing unusual was happening: these things must not be forgotten. After the terrible retreat was over, one man quietly remarked to me, "Well, it's been a bit of a mix-up, ain't it?" Such a spirit as that cannot be beaten.

I ask a prayer for the dear boys who will never return. May God Himself grant them everlasting peace, and a place at His right hand for evermore. I often think theirs is the happier part, and sometimes am selfishly inclined to envy them their great reward. But that is all as God wills. May He console the widowed, the orphan, and the desolate till the day breaks and the shadows flee away.

* * *

It is the third year since the Armistice. I had written more, but have not the heart to print it, so tear it up instead.

The England to which we have returned is so different from the England of our hopes and dreams; and when the boys say to me, "I am sorry I came back; I would be happier lying under a little white cross in France," what can I say, when I know it is true. If only the wonderful spirit of the trenches had been brought to England—but it has not. The world is more sordid and self-seeking than ever before.... " And we hoped that this had been He that should have Redeemed Israel, and besides it is the third day since these things were done." But no sacrifice can be in vain, and we trust where we cannot trace that "All is well, all shall be well, and He shall make all to be well." EXSPECTO RESURRECTIONEM MORTUORUM ET VITAM VENTURI SAECULI.

Index

A call to Brigade, 178
A day with 6th Batt. W.R.R. in the trenches at Nieuport, 25
Abeele, with the airmen at, 12
Advance through Méricourt l'Abbé, 143
After Passchendaele, a lunch at Poperinghe, 62
After the taking of Messines Ridge, 13
Albert, a shell on the road before, 109
Albert, first sight of, 81
Albert from the railway cutting, close view of, 141
All Saints' Day, at Steenvoorde, 65
All Saints' Day, Masses under fire, 173
Along the trenches at Nieuport, 32
Amiens–Albert Road, stirring days on the, 131
Amiens during the bombardment, 136
American doctor and wounded man, 59
American soldiers' first communion in the line, 139
American troops, first experience in the line of, 138
Amusing incident in the ward of C.C.S., 13
Anstaing, the reserve line at, 168
Armistice, first news of, 182
Attack on Nieuport abandoned, 43
Auchel, quiet days at, 161
Australian soldiers' retort, 134

Back to Bouzincourt, 118
Back to Bray dunes, 45
Back to the Menin Road, 78
Baizieux, machine-gunners caught at, 130
Bapaume–Péronne Road again, on the, 153
Bapaume–Péronne Road, scenes during the retreat, 107
Beauchamp during the great retreat, 100
Beaucourt, church bombed at, 129
Benediction in a pill-box at Passchendaele, 55
Bertincourt, "rest days" in, 88
Billet, burning of our, at Broxelle, 47
Blighty train, the, 11
Bombing around Albert, 109–10
Boulogne, arrival at, 2
Bourne, Cardinal, at Locre, 64

Bouzincourt, arrival at, 111
Boys who have not returned, the, 191
Bradley at Pernes, with Father, 129
Bradley, Father, a visit to, 63
Bray dunes, the march to, 21
Bridges at Nieuport, no loitering on the, 29
Burial by night at Franvillers, 136
Burial under fire at Nieuport, 35
Buried at Nieuport, Headquarters Staff, 31
Burying the dead near Morlancourt, 145
Buysscheure, exposition in church at, 46

Called to attend a military execution, 157
Cemetery at Remi siding, growth of the, 14
Charity towards enemy, the men's, 190
Charity, wonderful character of men's, 190
Cheerful start, a, up to the front line, 69
Christmas in Ribemont, 82
Cinema show, bombing of, at La Panne, 42
Contradiction of war, 10
Clearing Station, Casualty, 6
Cléry-sur-Somme, 155
Colonel's call to find food, 121
Communion, last, before going into Passchendaele, 51
Condemned soldier's death, 159
Confession and Communion on the front at Zonnebeke, 68
Cooks' prompt action after rough time, 121
Corcoran, Private, saves sacred vestments from Ribemont, 133
Courage of Territorial Sisters, 9
Coxyde, a conference at, 24
Crossing the Channel, 2
Crossing the Scheldt, 180

Dead, burying our last, 181
Desolation of the front at Ypres, 56–7
Digging out buried men in the Redan, 34
Dinner with Engineers in ramparts of Ypres, 53
Disappointment of those who have come back, 191

INDEX

Doctors, work of, in C.C.S., 10
Dominican convent in Froyennes, Sister Teresa protects, 174, 175
Dressing station at Nieuport, in the, 31
Drink, regulations for, 40
"Duke of Wellington's," first days with the, 17
Dunkerque, effects of long-range guns on, 21

Eaitch, Lieutenant, death of, 172
Earlsfield, farewell to, 1
Easter Day before Bouzincourt, 117
Endurance, our boys' splendid, 190
Enemy observation, keenness of, at Zonnebeke, 75
Equancourt, our little chapel at, 93
Esquerdes, a brief stay at, and a disappointment, 47
Evening at the C.C.S., 8
Exciting incident at Court of Inquiry, 52

Farewell to the Somme, 156
Feron's wonderful escape, Major, 172
Finding the 5th "Duke of Wellington's" at Passchendaele, 57
Fine work by German bearers, 152
Fins, incidents during the falling back on, 101
First American troops in the line, 138
First bombing of La Panne, 41
First coming of 17-inch shells in Nieuport, 36
First experience under fire, 4
First leave, 77
First sight of the line, 3
Flanagan, Lieutenant, death of, 147
Flanagan, Lieutenant, last talk with, 135
Folkestone during the War, 2
Foster's grave at La Neuville, Jack, 130
Fourth London Field Ambulance, 81
French peasants digging up their money under fire, 121
Fricourt, a whiz-bang at, 149

Gas casualties, 10
Gaston, Captain, death at Englebalmer, 124
German legends on abandoned dugouts, 141

"Girl's" courage at divisional show, 88
Going up the line near Cambrai, 83
Good-bye to the 49th Division, 80
Gordon, Father, death at Coxyde, 43
Gorringe, General, coolness in the line, 140
Greene's, Colonel, speech at Christmas dinner, 82
Guinness, Father, devoted work of, 59
Guns, sound of, quite home-like, 78

Half-way House, 67
Hardecourt, communion in action at, 151
Hell Fire Corner and Hell Blast Corner, 67
Henencourt Wood, meeting the Life Guards in, 137
Heroic work at Passchendaele, 61
Hilaire, St., out at rest in, 164
Hole made by 17-inch, Colonel Tew and, 37
Home for fourteen days, 77–8
Honnevain, a lively morning in, 170
Honnevain, death of Lieutenant Eaitch at, 171
Hospital, Father Murphy in, 77
Hot moments in Bouzincourt, 120
Hot time over Westhoek Ridge, 73

In the brickfield, 144
Inquiry into origin of fire at Broxelle, 50
Ironside in Henencourt, with Major, 141–2

Journey up the line to Nieuport, 25

Kennedy, General, at Ytres during the retreat, 105

La Panne, rest days at, 40, 41
Labour C.O. and padres, 17
Labour company near Hell Fire Corner, 71
Last days in the line at Nieuport, 34, 37
Last meeting with Lieutenants Simmons and Kent, 146
Last Sacraments to condemned soldier, 159
Last shells of the War, 179
Last sight of the battle front, 187–8

INDEX

Last talk with Captain Gaston, 120
Leave-train, the, 1
Lechelle, night at, 96
Lestrem, Mass at, and devotion of the people, 18
Lewis, General, consideration for Catholics, 20, 50
Lille, arrival before, 165
Lille, sufferings of the inhabitants of, 166
Lille, the great entry into, 166
Lorry, Sister Teresa finds a, at Bapaume, 91

Machine-gunners at Passchendaele, 55
Maloney, Father, blown up at Dickebusch, 15
Man's prayer when drowning in the Yser at Nieuport, 35
Marching out to rest at Abbeville, 128
Maricourt, days with Field Ambulance at, 90
Maricourt, the French chapel at, 90
Martinsart Wood, a night in, 115
Mass in Henencourt dressing station, 138
Mass of thanksgiving at La Tombe, 183
Menin Road, on the, 66
Men's gratitude for spiritual help, 189
Men's splendid comradeship in battle front, 188
Merville, after the German push at, 162
Messines Ridge, the artillery preparation, 7
Messines Ridge, the attack on, 12
Metz-en-Couture, 96
Mildren, General, at Ytres C.C.S., 104
Millencourt, a night in, 111
Moislains, the fight near, 153
Montgomery, Captain, courage of, at Nieuport, 34
Morning after relief at Nieuport, 39
Morning of the March Offensive, 1918, 97
Move to the sea, 20
Murphy, Father, endeavour to meet, 49
Murray Trench, a lively time in, 139

Narrow escape in streets of Nieuport, 36

Neeley, Colonel, in No Man's Land near Marcoing, 85
New Zealanders receive Communion in action, 58
Nieuport, first mustard gas attack at, 22
Night of the Armistice, solemnity and silence of the, 183

Old friend at Englebalmer, meeting with an, 117
Ordish, in the line with Captain, 87

Paradis, Mass with the "Duke of Wellington's" at, 19
Passion Sunday at Equancourt and Vallulart Wood, 94
Patience of wounded in hospital, 8
Péronne, a day in, 92
Petrol dump blown up, 112
Pleasant quarters at Coxyde, 30
Poperinghe, 4
Preparing a condemned soldier for death, 158
Protection near Senlis, Sister Teresa's, 124

Quartes, a rest with the curé at, 181

Rancourt, capture of, 152
Red Rose Camp, 52
Redmond, Major Willie, at the grave at Locre, 64
Relief at Bouzincourt, Lieutenant Brown and the, 125
Relief at Nieuport, 39
Remi siding, arrival at, 4
Reorganisation of army, indignation at, 89
Reported killed, Father Murphy, 63
Retiring for Villas Pluich, 100
Ribecourt, resting in, 86
Rocquigny, the retirement through, 105
Royal Welsh near Rancourt, 154
R.T.O.s, Army's opinion of, 16
Rubber House, the, in the Redan at Nieuport, 26
Rumours of the end, 176

St. Omer, the R.T.O. at, 63
St. Pol-sur-la-Mer, Mass and Communion at, 20
Saving church vestments in Bouzincourt, 119
Senlis, a heavy morning in, 123

Shell fire, under, before Abraham's Heights, 57
Shell spoils brigade dinner, 142
Shell, the first, in La Panne, 43
Shells at Nieuport, 4·2 to 17·0, 28
Shelter at Nieuport, prayer in a, 27
Shelter in Martinsart Wood, a new, 116
Shy penitent at Ypres, 75
Silent walks over the Somme valley, 91
Smithers, Captain, soldiers' opinion of, 131
Soldiers' opinion of the Somme people, 128
Steenvoorde, quiet days in, 65
Syon Abbey, a rush to, 78

Te Deum in Tournai Cathedral, 184
Tent, the disadvantages of, 21
Teresa, Sister's, intervention going into the line, 84
Territorial Sisters, devoted work of, 9
Tew, Colonel, character of, 19
Tew, Colonel, leaves battalion at La Panne, 43

Vespers at Teteghem, 45

Waiting to go home, 186
Walker, Major, and the padre's daily task, 39
Warloy, Mass on Good Friday in, 114
Warloy, with the Labour Company at, 130
Warm moment on Menin Road, 70
Warmhoudt, day at, 45
Watou, Mass at, 51
Way up to Passchendaele, 54
Weeks', Captain, devoted work at Nieuport, 33
Welsh Ridge, incident on, 87
When the War is over, French girl's opinion of, 187
Why the Town Major moved at Coxyde, 30
Wieltje, burial under difficulties at, 53
Wieltje, headquarters in mine shaft at, 52
Winnezeele, in rest at, 64
Wonderful escape from bomb at La Panne, 43
Work around La Panne, 44
Work in the Somme valley, 93
Wounded at Passchendaele, Father Murphy, 63

X Camp, a bomb in, 62
X Camp, experiences in, 61–2

Young doctor's first experience in the line at Nieuport, 34
Ypres, Mass in, 76
Ytres, a night in the C.C.S. at, 89
Ytres evacuated, 103

Zelobes, days with the Field Ambulance at, 17

Printed in England for the Ambrosden Press by Hazell, Watson & Viney, Ld., London and Aylesbury.

www.ingramcontent.com/pod-product-compliance
Lightning Source LLC
Chambersburg PA
CBHW031953080426
42735CB00007B/379